KU-497-156

Table of Contents

Why Wireless Networking? 7

Who Needs a Home Network? 8
Why Go Wireless? 9
Wireless Networking Basics 10
Wireless Networking Options 12
What You'll Find in this Book 16

Wireless Networking Components 17

Which Wireless Networking Standard? 18
Wireless Network Components 20
Wireless Network Adapters for PCs 21
Access Points for Wireless Home Networks 24
Wireless Network Adapters for Other Devices 26
Wireless Home Media Servers 27

Your First Wireless Home Network 29

Introduction 30
Installing a Wireless Network Adapter in Windows 98/2000/ME 31
Installing a Wireless Network Adapter in Windows XP 35
Connecting to a Peer-to-Peer Wireless Network 37
Creating a New Peer-to-Peer Wireless Network 39
Maintaining Security on Peer-to-Peer Wireless Networks 41

Sharing Network Resources 45

Network Setup Using Windows XP   46
Sharing Files and Folders   51
Sharing a Printer   53
Sharing a Drive   55
My Network Places   58
Network Protocols and Services   60
Internet Protocol Addressing   62

From Networking to Internetworking 65

Introduction   66
Setting up an Infrastructure Mode Wireless Home Network   67
Locating Your Access Point   68
Installing the Router and Configuring Network PCs   69
Access Point / Router Configuration   71
Additional Configuration Options   77

Internet Connections and Firewalls 83

Internet Connection Sharing   84
Managing a Shared Internet Connection   86
Using Windows Firewall   88
Remote Access to Your Wireless Home Network   93

Managing Your Wireless Network 97

Monitoring Network Performance   98
Backing Up Your Network Data   101
Running the Windows XP Backup Utility   103
Advanced Backup Options   106

WIRELESS HOME NETWORKING

STEVE RACKLEY

In easy steps is an imprint of Computer Step
Southfield Road . Southam
Warwickshire CV47 0FB . United Kingdom
www.ineasysteps.com

Notice of Liability
Every effort has been made to ensure that this book contains accurate
and current information. However, Computer Step and the author
shall not be liable for any loss or damage suffered by readers as a
result of any information contained herein.

Acknowledgements and Trademarks
Product images courtesy of Sony Corp., Philips Consumer
Electronics, IOGEAR Inc., Hewlett-Packard Company, Cisco
Systems Inc. (including Linksys), Buffalo Technology Inc.
and ANYCOM Technologies GmbH.

All trademarks are acknowledged as belonging to their respective
companies.

Printed and bound in the United Kingdom

ISBN-13 978-1-84078-289-9
ISBN-10 1-84078-289-7

Completing the Backup   108
Restoring Backed Up Network Data   109
Advanced Restore Options   111
Completing the Restore   112

Securing Your Wireless Network   113

Threats to Wireless Security   114
What's at Stake?   115
Wireless Security Best Practice   116
Wi-Fi Protected Access (WPA)   119
Downloading Windows XP Service Pack Updates   120
Installing Windows XP Service Pack Updates   122
Updating Wireless Adapter Drivers for WPA   124
Securing Remote Network Access   127

Extending Wireless Network Range   129

Why Worry About Range?   130
Making the Most of What You've Got   131
Using an External Antenna to Increase Range   132
Do-It-Yourself Antennas   134
Wireless Network Bridging   136
Community Wireless   138

Wireless Hotspot Networking   141

Introducing Wireless Hotspots   142
Finding a Hotspot   143
Connecting to Hotspot Services   144
Hotspots in the USA and Canada   145
Hotspots in the UK and Europe   149

International Hotspots 152

Hotspot Security 154

Troubleshooting Your Home Network 157

First Analyze the Problem 158

Troubleshooting Network Adapters 160

Troubleshooting Network Resource Hosts 162

Troubleshooting Network Connections 163

Wireless Interference 164

Troubleshooting Internet Connection Sharing 165

If Wireless Zero Configuration is Not Available 166

Checking Network Connectivity 168

Other DOS Diagnostic Tools 171

Diagnostics Using MS Help and Support Center 173

Further Information Sources 175

General Networking 176

Wireless Networking 178

Hotspot Directories 180

Community Wireless 181

General Wireless Topics 182

Offbeat Wireless Topics 183

Buying Wireless Home Network Gear 184

Network Troubleshooting 185

Index 187

Why Wireless Networking?

In this introductory chapter we'll look at the main reasons for starting out on home networking, and at the advantages of going wireless. We'll take a very quick look under the hood, just to get to know the bare minimum of technicalities, and then we'll look at the various options that are available for setting up a wireless home network.

Finally we'll run through the key steps that we'll be covering later in the book as you build your wireless home network.

Covers

Who Needs a Home Network? | 8

Why Go Wireless? | 9

Wireless Networking Basics | 10

Wireless Networking Options | 12

What You'll Find in this Book | 16

Chapter One

Who Needs a Home Network?

Until recently, the business of network adapters, IP addressing and configuring network connections was only for the most adept of home computer users, and the rest of us were left scratching our heads when we needed to transfer a file bigger than a 1.4 MB floppy from one computer to another.

Now all that's changed. Not only is it easier than ever to set up a home network, but you can now do it just as easily without wires.

And none too soon either! Gone are the days when the family's sole PC took an honoured place in the corner of the den or study; now they're also in the kids' bedrooms, for homework as well as games. Now there's a queue to use the main PC too, for email, Web surfing and the like, and it's even more of a bottleneck because it also runs the printer, scanner and other gear as well as the Internet connection.

A home network can also give a new lease of life to that old computer you were about to recycle. It may not have the speed, but once hooked up in your network it will be able to share resources like mass storage or the DVD-RW with your latest hot laptop.

Enter the Network

Into this increasingly complex scene comes the network, a solution that delivers easy shared access to all the family's home computing resources. No more need to wait for the kids' homework to be done before you can check your email.

A home network will allow every computer in your home to access the Internet connection, printer and other resources. You'll be able to open up files on one machine from another and share storage devices like hard drives or DVD-ROMs. Streaming digital media such as audio and video from computer to computer, or to your Hi-Fi or TV might also be on your wants list.

Networking in Windows XP SP2

Windows XP takes a lot of the hard work out of setting up and running a home network because it was specifically developed with networking in mind. And with Windows XP SP2, that ease extends to wireless home networks too, with new easy-to-use connection and setup tools and wizards.

Networking is now a realistic option for the average home computer user, without the need for advanced computer skills. That's not a guarantee that it's all going to be problem free of course, but this book will make the steps to set up your first wireless home network as easy as they possibly can be!

Why Go Wireless?

The key standards are 802.11b, also known as Wi-Fi, and 802.11g, known as Wi-Fi5. These standards are developed by the Institute of Electrical and Electronics Engineers, the IEEE.

Wireless networking has taken off in the last few years as a result of the development of industry standards that encouraged the development and ensured the interoperability of equipment from a growing list of different manufacturers.

Coupled with this there have been continuing dramatic price reductions on the microchip sets that drive wireless hardware and, both in the US and in Europe, decreasing regulation of the radio frequency spectrum used for wireless networking.

Wireless advantages

In the home, going wireless has two main advantages, both of which are pretty obvious.

There are also some "no new wires" options that use existing cabling in your home. We'll have a look at these on page 12.

Firstly you don't need all those cables, so wireless is a lot more partner friendly than wired networking! No need to drill holes through walls for cables and sockets. No crouching in dusty loft spaces laying cable runs out of sight, or time spent redecorating afterwards.

The second advantage is the total flexibility of wireless – you won't be tied down to a few locations that you have been able to wire up. If you want to install a new computer in another room you can leave the toolbox in the garage. If you want to move out of doors and check your email, surf the net or work online, all you need is a laptop and a wireless adapter and you can sit on the deck or in an easy chair beside the pool.

... and limitation

When you leave the wires behind, security becomes an important issue, because it's much easier to snoop on a radio signal than on data flowing in a network cable. But ensuring the security of your wireless home network is not complex and we'll cover the essential security steps to achieve this in chapter 8.

Rise of the mobile worker

The flexibility of going wireless is not just limited to sharing resources and Internet connections in and around the home. With a wireless enabled laptop you'll be able to connect to the Internet wirelessly at an increasing number of so-called "hotspots", in coffee shops, hotels, airport lounges and conference centers.

Hotspots are covered in chapter 10.

Wireless Networking Basics

Fortunately it's not necessary to understand the technologies that make networks work – whether wired or wireless – in order to get your own wireless home network up and running. Nevertheless, to enable you to get the best out of your network, and to be able to avoid some of the pitfalls that could cause problems later on, we'll spend a few minutes getting a few of the basics of wireless networking out of the way.

Network connections and data flow

The business of getting a piece of data, like an email message, from one computer to another relies on a lot of hidden activity behind the scenes. At the heart of networking there are a number of standards and protocols that control how connections (or sessions) are set up between computers, how data is broken down into packets, routed from one computer to another (whether within a room or across the globe) and then reassembled.

A protocol is a set of definitions and rules that specify how these various activities are organized and how they interoperate within a network.

At this level of establishing connections and controlling data flow, wired and wireless networks work in exactly the same way. These functions are managed by various pieces of software on your computer, primarily by the operating system. As we noted before, operating systems like Windows XP are designed to make networking easy, so we won't have to pay too much attention to these aspects of networking.

The devices that access the physical network medium are called network adapters. We'll look at these in the next chapter.

The real difference between wired and wireless only comes into play when we get down to the level of the physical communication medium (wires versus radio waves) and the way in which devices access and share the medium.

Data rate

When we look at various networking options in the next section, we'll talk about the data rate that can be achieved, and the units of Mbps or million bits per second will come into the discussion. We'll see that hardware for home networking typically achieves data rates in the 10 Mbps to 100 Mbps range.

Remember that a byte has 8 bits, so a 1 MB file has 8 Mb of data to be transmitted. In fact the data is broken into packets for transmission which means you end up transmitting quite a lot more data to control this process.

For most home applications, the only time you'll feel a limitation at the bottom end of this range is when you're transferring large files between computers. Your broadband Internet connection will

Remember that Kbps is kilo- or thousand-bps, so 1 Mbps is equal to 1000 Kbps.

probably be running at between 256 Kbps and 1.5 Mbps, so that will not be troubled by a 10 Mbps network.

If one of your networking requirements is the ability to stream digital media such as video around the home then you will need to be aiming for network speeds of at least 50 Mbps.

Radio frequency spectrum

We tend to think of "wireless" as synonymous with radio, but there are a number of different ways you can make your home network "wireless" and we will look at these in the next section. However, most of this book will be concerned with Wi-Fi or Wi-Fi5 systems that use radio waves as the physical link between computers.

Wi-Fi and Wi-Fi5 have a lot in common with the radio frequency transmissions used by cell phones, but unlike these networks, wireless networking hardware transmits at RF frequencies that are unlicensed, which means that you don't need to get a radio operator's license to transmit data over a home network!

However, because it is unlicensed, it does mean that there are a lot of other appliances out there using the same frequencies. Cordless phones in the home, garage door remote controllers and also the common microwave oven are all potential sources of interference, as we shall see in chapters 9 and 11.

Transmitters, antennas and receivers

Although Wi-Fi and Wi-Fi5 frequency bands are unlicensed, the regulatory authorities do put limits on the way these bands can be used. For example, a maximum transmitter power of 1 Watt is specified in the USA (it's 0.1 Watt in Europe). At the other end, the sensitivity of the receiver is dictated by fundamental physical noise limits.

A wireless network adapter has a radio transmitter, antenna and receiver packaged together with the circuitry to code and decode data onto the radio signal.

Because of these limitations, and because radio frequency signals are attenuated by walls, floors/ceilings and other obstacles, it's important to make the most of the power available from your hardware. We'll look at the steps you can take to get maximum performance from your hardware, such as using external antennas, in chapter 9.

Wireless Networking Options

So, you've decided that your home needs a network and that the last thing you need is the hassle of routing cables around the place. A wireless home network is the answer.

Although Wi-Fi and Wi-Fi5 are the solutions that we'll spend most of this book describing, there are a number of alternatives that you should consider before deciding what's right for you. We'll look at some of these options, and the pros and cons of each, in this section.

No More Wires options

Before we look at going truly wireless, you should consider another option for home networking that also leaves the drill in your toolbox. "No More Wires" is a phrase that has been coined to refer to networks that use existing cabling such as phone or power lines as the physical connection medium.

HomePNA stands for the Home Phoneline Networking Alliance. See chapter 12 for sources of information on the hardware manufacturers for these various standards.

The two main standards are HomePNA, using existing phone lines, and HomePlug, using existing electrical power cabling, and a number of manufacturers produce hardware to these standards for home networking.

A HomePNA compatible USB network adapter giving data rates up to 10 Mbps over your existing phone lines

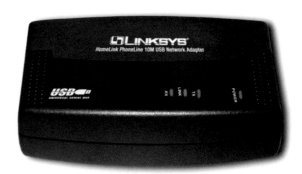

The HomePNA specification is also better suited than Wi-Fi and Wi-Fi5 for streaming real-time data such as video, since it ensures that the data packets arrive in the order they are required.

The HomePNA 3.0 standard finalized in 2003 enables data rates of 128 Mbps, with the possibility of reaching 240 Mbps. As we'll see later, this is well above current wireless specifications. If your home networking objective is to stream digital media such as audio and video between fixed locations then this could be the solution for your wireless (or at least no new wires!) home network.

HomePNA has the disadvantage that not every room in the home has a phone socket, but every room has one or more power sockets, so HomePlug has the edge in offering a higher degree of flexibility as far as location is concerned.

HomePlug hardware is made by several manufacturers, including Linksys, Netgear and SMC. Find out more about networking using HomePlug at www.homeplug.org.

A HomePlug
Ethernet bridge
can connect a wired
network device such as a
broadband modem into a home
powerline network

Data rates up to 14 Mbps mean that HomePlug is as fast as or faster than Wi-Fi, but the main limitation is in terms of mobility. For a desktop machine, which is tied to a power outlet, HomePlug may be a good option.

HomePlug is also being actively developed, with Asoka and Bell South collaborating to develop 85Mbps hardware.

But if you want your laptop to have complete mobility around the home, then carrying an AC adapter together with a HomePlug adapter may be a bit too cumbersome. Either way, if you want your home network to extend over a range of several hundred feet, then a hybrid network including HomePlug alongside Wi-Fi will be an option to consider.

Infrared connections

Many devices these days, from PCs to PDAs, digital cameras and mobile phones include an infrared (IR) port that can be used to connect to other compatible devices. It is also possible to buy an external IR port that can connect to your computer, printer or other peripheral via a USB port.

The most common standard for connecting devices using infrared is called IrDA (Infrared Data Association). Make sure you check devices for compatibility. Find out more at www.irda.org.

An IR connection allows simple data transfer between devices and is an easy way of moving a few files around. The main limitation is the lack of physical flexibility. You need to have a direct line-of-sight between the transmitting and receiving ports and the effective range is limited to about three to six feet (one to two

To check whether your computer has an IR port click Start, Control Panel or Start, Settings, Control Panel and see whether there is an Infrared item in your Control Panel.

meters). Unlike radio based systems, an IR link will not get you into the next room, or out into the garden!

The speed of data transfer over an IR link is also much less than over Wi-Fi: IrDA will get you anything from 100 Kbps to 4 Mbps, compared to 11 Mbps for Wi-Fi and 54 Mbps for Wi-Fi5.

Bluetooth

Bluetooth is a radio based wireless system that, like IrDA, is intended to work over a fairly short range, in this case up to about 30 feet (10 meters). The goal of Bluetooth is easy connectivity between personal devices, such as a mobile phone, headset and PDA to form a so-called Personal Area Network or PAN.

A Personal Area Network (PAN) is in contrast to a Local Area Network (LAN), which typically links together several computers and peripherals over an extended area such as a home or office.

A Bluetooth printer adapter will allow any Bluetooth enabled PDA, computer or other device to send files to a printer. In this case both parallel and USB printer connections are available

Up to eight devices can be connected in a Bluetooth PAN, with data rates of up to 730 Kbps, and the nominal 30 foot (10 meter) range can be extended using external amplifiers. Bluetooth devices are typically Plug-n-Play, which means that you don't have to worry about installing special drivers – just plug it into the device and you're ready to go!

Although a range of 30 feet (10 meters) is usually quoted for Bluetooth devices, up to 300 feet (100 meters) can be achieved under ideal circumstances.

A Bluetooth PAN can also be interconnected to a wired or wireless Local Area Network or LAN, using a bridging device such as the Anycom AP-2002 shown on the next page. Bridging into a LAN will allow Bluetooth devices to access other network resources as well as connect to the Internet. Setting up a Bluetooth access point

Bluetooth and Wi-Fi share the same unlicensed RF band. They are designed to work alongside each other, but some interference may occur.

A Bluetooth access point will allow any Bluetooth enabled PDA, computer or other device to connect to a network

Network access, control and security features can be configured, using a simple web browser interface.

like this is similar to the process for a Wi-Fi access point that we will be covering in chapter 5.

HomeRF

HomeRF was a home wireless networking standard that had many similarities to Wi-Fi, but has now been completely overtaken by the Wi-Fi explosion. As well as basic wireless networking, HomeRF promised additional features such as integrating with cordless phones, priority assignment to data packets, and low power requirements so that PDAs and similar devices could use it as an alternative to Bluetooth.

... and finally, Wi-Fi

Last, but not least, comes Wi-Fi and its high speed sibling Wi-Fi5. As the most popular solution for wireless home networking, Wi-Fi offers a wide range of hardware options, from a long list of manufacturers. Data speeds of 11 Mbps for Wi-Fi, 54 Mbps for Wi-Fi5, the promise of higher rates in the future and at least a degree of backward compatibility will make this the obvious choice for most wireless home networks.

If you don't want to be tied to a phone line or power cable, and have no intention of getting the toolbox out to run new cabling in your home, then the chances are this is a good choice for you. In the next chapter we'll look at the pros and cons of the different flavors of Wi-Fi.

What You'll Find in this Book

Later chapters in this book will take you progressively through the key stages of selecting, installing and configuring your wireless home network. Of course if there's one topic you want to start on, perhaps hotspot networking (chapter 10), then jump right in there! If not, then here is an outline of how the topics will develop as we progress through the book.

- In chapter 2 we take a look at the various wireless networking standards that are available and the hardware components you'll need to build your wireless home network

- In chapter 3 we'll cover setting up your first wireless home network, a simple computer-to-computer connection

- In chapter 4 you'll discover how to set up files, printers, drives and other resources to be shared over the network

- We'll set-up a fully fledged network in chapter 5 with a wireless access point and Internet connection

- Chapter 6 will take us through setting up, managing and protecting the Internet connection to your network

- We'll look at a few network management tasks in chapter 7, including data backup, that will keep your network in top shape

- In chapter 8 we'll deal with the important issue of how to keep your wireless home network secure

- Extending the range of your wireless network will be covered in chapter 9, including a look at DIY antennas and community wireless networks

- Then chapter 10 will introduce the exciting world of connecting to the Internet using wireless hotspots

- Troubleshooting common problems, both at the network level and specifically for the wireless link will be covered in chapter 11

- Finally, chapter 12 introduces a range of additional information sources that will help broaden your knowledge of home wireless networking and keep you in touch with future developments

Wireless Networking Components

In this chapter we'll look at the components you'll need to get your wireless home network going. First we'll run through the three varieties of Wi-Fi equipment that are available today, and set out the pros and cons to help you make the right choice for your network.

Then we'll look at wireless network adapters for PCs, access points for building out your network, and wireless adapters for connecting other types of hardware to your Wi-Fi network.

Finally we'll look at some specific hardware options that you'll want to consider if digital media streaming is an objective for your wireless home network.

Chapter Two

Covers

Which Wireless Networking Standard? | 18

Wireless Network Components | 20

Wireless Network Adapters for PCs | 21

Access Points for Wireless Home Networks | 24

Wireless Network Adapters for Other Devices | 26

Wireless Home Media Servers | 27

Which Wireless Networking Standard?

Having looked at various alternative wireless (or nearly wireless) networking solutions in the last chapter, we're now homing in on Wi-Fi and the different versions of this, the most popular home wireless networking solution.

Wi-Fi has been evolving rapidly in the last few years, and the most widely available "common or garden" variety – the original classic Wi-Fi – has now been supplemented by two new faster versions.

IEEE stands for the Institute of Electrical and Electronics Engineers.

These varieties of Wi-Fi refer to systems that are based on different versions of the IEEE 802.11 standard. This standard, which defines the ways in which the wireless end of wireless networking hardware operates, now has three "flavors": a, b and g. Let's take a look at these options.

Wi-Fi "Classic"

Wi-Fi is short for Wireless Fidelity and is the name coined by the Wi-Fi Alliance to indicate 802.11 based wireless network systems. You can find out more about the Wi-Fi Alliance at www.wi-fi.org.

The original Wi-Fi "classic" is based on the IEEE 802.11b version of the Wi-Fi standard. This has been around the longest and therefore has the greatest variety of hardware available, from a wide range of manufacturers.

It was also the simplest and cheapest of the three varieties to implement, which is why it hit the streets before its alphabetically earlier sibling 802.11a – more of which later.

ISM stands for Instrument, Scientific and Medical – so no prizes for guessing the uses that the spectrum regulators intended for these slices of radio frequency real estate.

Classic Wi-Fi delivers data speeds of up to 11 Mbps, plenty for most file transfer type network usage. It operates on the so-called ISM radio band at 2.4 GHz, which it shares with a plethora of other devices from cordless phones to garage door remote controls. So interference can be a problem with this Wi-Fi variety if your household has a lot of this type of gadget.

On the other hand, since it's now been around a while, and there are a lot of manufacturers competing for your attention, classic Wi-Fi hardware is the least expensive of the three.

More speed with g

The next variety, based on the 802.11g version of the Wi-Fi standard, brings a dramatic increase in speed – now up to 54 Mbps – which is fast enough to make real-time video streaming a

As you would expect, if you operate 802.11b equipment in an 802.11g network, the computer with the b adapter will not be able to work at the speed of g!

And of course it doesn't stop here. Already in the pipeline, 802.11n looks set to give a further ramp up in speed to 108 Mbps, and possibly to 320 Mbps in the next couple of years.

possibility. 802.11g equipment runs on the same ISM band as Wi-Fi classic, so if interference is going to be a problem it will be with 802.11g as well. On the plus side, as well as the healthy dose of data speed, 802.11g is backwards compatible with 802.11b, which means that 802.11b equipment can operate in an 802.11g network.

Wi-Fi5

The last of the three Wi-Fi flavors is based on the 802.11a version of the IEEE standard. Here we have a significant change in that Wi-Fi5 operates on a different radio band from b and g. In this case it's an ISM band at 5 GHz (hence the 5 in Wi-Fi5). This is a much less crowded piece of radio spectrum, so interference is less likely to be a problem (at least for now!)

As far as data speed goes, Wi-Fi5 equals the best of its siblings, also delivering 54 Mbps.

The choice is yours ...

So the factors that will influence your choice are cost, speed and whether your home is likely to be a high interference environment for a wireless network to operate in.

Classic Wi-Fi will give you the cheapest option, with a wide range of equipment available, and probably a lot of good second-hand equipment available, for example on eBay, from early adopters who are now trading up to 802.11a or g. A data speed of up to 11 Mbps will be fine for most applications.

All three versions of Wi-Fi are similar in terms of achievable range, since the maximum allowable power is the same for all three. Theoretically Wi-Fi5 should have a slightly lower range in view of its higher transmitting frequency, but this is often hard to spot in practice.

If data speed is your major consideration, then 802.11g is probably the choice for you. Because of its backwards compatibility, you will also be able to take advantage of less expensive classic 802.11b hardware for those parts of your wireless network where speed is not of the essence.

If your household is full of wireless gadgets then you might want to consider Wi-Fi5. On the other hand you might want to try out a classic Wi-Fi network first, maybe by borrowing some equipment from a friend. The other gadgets around your home are probably not in use all the time, so interference may not pose too much of a problem.

Wireless Network Components

To build a wireless network to connect a number of computers and peripherals around your home you need just two essential hardware components.

Wireless network adapters

The first is the wireless network adapter, which gives each individual computer or other device the ability to use wireless signals as a physical communication medium. In the next section we'll look at the wide range of different types of wireless network adapter that are available.

Wireless access points

The simplest type of wireless connection is a computer-to-computer link, also known as a peer-to-peer or ad hoc network. We'll look at this type of connection in chapter 3.

The second component, which is essential for all but the simplest wireless networks, is the wireless access point (or AP). This will be the hub of your wireless network, and will coordinate wireless communication between the various networked devices.

In a stand-alone wireless network, without an Internet connection, your access point can be connected directly to your main PC using a wired Ethernet connection, in which case this PC will not need a separate wireless network adapter.

Additional AP functions – switching and routing

We'll look more at access point capabilities later in this chapter.

Access points for wireless home networking generally provide a range of additional functions, two of which are routing and switching.

If your wireless network includes an always-on Internet connection, then your access point can be wired directly to your DSL or cable modem as well as to your main PC. The access point's routing function will manage traffic between the Internet and the computers in your network, whether wired or wireless.

If you want to combine wired and wireless components in your home network, many access points include a number of Ethernet sockets as well as the switch function that directs wired network traffic to the intended destination within your network.

Now we'll take a look at the available range of hardware components and their capabilities in a little more detail.

Wireless Network Adapters for PCs

The first component you need to get started with wireless networking is the network adapter.

Wireless network adapters for laptop PCs

The standard wireless network adapter for a laptop is an internal adapter that slots into a free PC slot on the side of your laptop. Here is a typical example.

If your PC slots are all occupied, you can also use a USB wireless adapter for your laptop.

This type of adapter has an internal radio antenna, housed inside the bulbous end of the adapter that sticks out at the side of the laptop. If you think you might want to extend the range of your network then consider buying an adapter with a connector to attach an external antenna. An example of this type is shown here.

Extending the range of your wireless network is covered in chapter 9.

Connector to attach external antenna

Look out for the Wi-Fi Alliance's mark on your Wi-Fi gear to ensure interoperability with other manufacturers.

Installing a laptop network adapter requires little more than sliding it into the spare PC slot. Software installation and setup will be covered in chapter 3.

Wireless network adapters for desktop PCs

There are two basic types of wireless network adapter for desktop computers: internal and external.

An internal adapter, such as the example shown here, occupies a spare PCI slot inside your computer

Internal adapters have the advantage that the antenna is often attached to the card using a removable connector. This allows an external antenna to be attached if you want to extend the range of your network.

Installation of an internal adapter is straightforward.

Make sure to turn the power off before you open the housing of your PC!

1   Open the housing of your PC – usually the side for a tower type housing or otherwise the top

2   Locate a spare PCI slot and unscrew the small cover plate. Be careful not to lose the screw!

3   Slide your network adapter into the free slot and retain it in place using the same screw. Refit the side/top of your PC housing

We'll cover the installation of software drivers and setting up the adapter in the next chapter.

Another type of internal adapter for a desktop computer allows you to slot a laptop PC wireless adapter, such as those shown on page 21, into a desktop PCI slot.

With this type of internal adapter you could economize and use a single PC card for both your laptop and desktop, although it's not much use if you want to wirelessly connect the two together!

A final type of adapter that you can use for both laptop and desktop machines is the USB adapter.

The USB type of adapter comes in a variety of types, and can be used equally well to connect a desktop or a laptop computer to your wireless home network.

Since USB devices can be "daisy-chained", you can plug this type of adapter into any available USB port on your system, for example on your monitor, or on another USB device. It does not have to be connected to a USB port directly on your computer.

Access Points for Wireless Home Networks

We'll learn about these network functions in the following chapters.

The access point, or AP, is the main component of most wireless home networks. Access points come in a variety of different configurations from a relatively simple device that bridges between wired and wireless networks, to full-featured APs that combine several different network functions such as switching, routing and print serving, and may even include a broadband modem.

Access point as a simple wireless hub

Some APs also include a printer server feature, allowing a printer to be shared without the need for a host PC to be switched on.

If your goal is simply to provide a hub for a number of wireless enabled computers to connect to an existing wired network then a simple access point such as the one shown here will do the job.

A basic AP will also give you wireless bridging capabilities to extend the range of your network. See page 136 for wireless bridging.

This type of access point will allow any wireless enabled computer to connect to the wired network and access shared resources. The role of the access point is simply to transmit and receive wireless broadcast signals and to translate between wired and wireless modes of communication.

Check out sites like wi-fiplanet (see page 182) for info and reviews of all the latest gear.

Access point as an Internet gateway

If an objective of your network is to wirelessly share an Internet connection, then your access point can also be the gateway through which wireless enabled computers will connect to the Internet.

A combined access point/gateway such as the one shown here will provide network routing and usually allows several wired network connections through an integrated multi-port Ethernet switch.

Access point as a network bridge

An additional capability that we will look at in chapter 9 is wireless network bridging. In this configuration, two or more access points are used to link or bridge between separated wired networks.

If you expect your network to extend beyond the range of a single access point, beyond say a few hundred feet, you may want to include wireless bridging capabilities in your selection criteria when deciding which access point is right for your wireless home network.

Access point as the ultimate network component

If you have a DSL or cable modem providing your broadband Internet connection, you can also find access points that include this function and can replace your existing modem – if you're very keen to eliminate unnecessary boxes under your computer desk.

Wireless hub, wired network switch, Internet gateway, network bridge, broadband modem, print server – it seems there is no end to the capabilities that manufacturers can bundle into this ultimate network component!

Wireless Network Adapters for Other Devices

Once you've got your wireless network up and running, you'll soon want to hook up some of your other devices around the home. The flexibility of your wireless home network can easily be extended to include a variety of other capabilities.

A games adapter will allow you to wirelessly connect a network ready games console for wireless Internet gaming or head-to-head gaming between two or more consoles anywhere within range of your network.

We'll cover Port Forwarding, a little technicality that you'll need for online gaming, in chapter 5.

An 802.11g games adapter from Linksys

A wireless enabled video camera will allow you to keep an eye on your home security from anywhere you can access the Internet.

This example includes an integrated web server – it can connect directly to the Internet without needing a host PC

A wireless music system will let you hear the music collection from your PC via the full power of your stereo system, or use the built-in speakers to play it anywhere around the house.

Linksys 802.11b music system

Wireless Home Media Servers

Wi-Fi meets the home cinema

Since Wi-Fi's speedy variant 802.11g was approved by the IEEE in June 2003, wireless home networking hardware with the speed to stream video between devices such as DVDs, TVs and PCs has become available.

This opens up the possibility of delivering video and other digital media content anywhere in the home from a single central point, and controlling this delivery using a single interface. Enter the home media server.

Sony RoomLink

Until standards mature, expect many of these devices to have proprietary interfaces, which may not work with other manufacturers' equipment. Sony's RoomLink, for example, will only work with Sony PCs.

Major consumer electronics companies like Sony (RoomLink), Panasonic (AVC Server) and Philips (Streamium) are marketing devices to act as a bridge for digital content between a PC, network attached storage, DVDs, and TVs or Hi-Fi systems.

Philips iPronto

Controlling these devices will be a new breed of remote control, like the one shown here, which will enable you to operate your entertainment system, access your PC and surf the Internet all from one stylish interface.

A PC by any other name ...

But before considering special-purpose media server equipment, let's realize that most of the capabilities that are required here will already be in your wireless home network – in your PC!

And that's why Microsoft and the PC manufacturers are focusing on this aspect and fine tuning the digital media serving capabilities of the PC and its operating system, rather than expecting us to buy more hardware – after all, the purpose of a central server is to reduce the number of boxes scattered around the home, not to add to it.

Microsoft's Windows XP Media Center Edition has been designed to enable the convergence of PC and home entertainment technologies. Media Center PCs, being marketed by Dell, Toshiba and others, with Windows XP Media Center installed, can connect directly to a standard or widescreen TV and deliver standard PC functions as well as new media services like personal video recording (PVR) using an online Electronic Program Guide (EPG). So, if streaming video and digital movies are an objective of your network, take a look at Media Center PCs and the latest version of Windows XP.

Personal Video recording (PVR) allows you to record up to three simultaneous TV programs while using your Media Center PC for normal PC functions.

The one additional hardware component you'll need is an adapter to link the other TVs around your home into your wireless network.

It's built to look at home in the living room rather than the study, but at heart this unit from Linksys is simply a wireless network adapter for your TV!

As we noted earlier in this chapter, you'll need to build your network on 802.11a or 802.11g hardware if you want to have the data speed for handling video and TV signals.

Now that we've had a good look at the hardware components you'll need to get your wireless home network up and running, and extend it to a range of devices around the home, it's time to get things moving and set up your first wireless network.

Your First Wireless Home Network

In this chapter you'll find out how to set up your first wireless home network – a simple connection between two wireless enabled computers, also known as a peer-to-peer connection. We'll look at installing the wireless network adapters into a laptop or desktop computer and either connecting to an existing peer-to-peer wireless connection or setting up a new one.

Finally we'll run through the key steps that you'll need to take to maintain security on your first wireless home network.

Covers

Introduction | 30

Installing a Wireless Network Adapter
in Windows 98/2000/ME | 31

Installing a Wireless Network Adapter in Windows XP | 35

Connecting to a Peer-to-Peer Wireless Network | 37

Creating a New Peer-to-Peer Wireless Network | 39

Maintaining Security on Peer-to-Peer Wireless Networks | 41

Chapter Three

Introduction

In the coming pages we will learn how to install wireless network adapters and connect two or more computers in a simple network to share files or other resources.

This type of connection is known as a peer-to-peer or ad hoc network, and is one of two varieties of wireless link that are defined in the Wi-Fi or 802.11 wireless network standard.

The other type of connection, called infrastructure mode, is covered in chapter 5.

Windows XP includes a service called Zero Configuration which enables automatic switching between network modes. Check your chosen adapter for Windows XP compatibility to ensure this feature is available.

A peer-to-peer network connecting several computers, which could be desktops, laptops, PDAs or other wireless network ready home electronic devices

Each of the computers in a peer-to-peer network communicates equally with all other computers in the network, without any central hub or access point to direct network traffic.

Network communication is a multi-level process, and setting up a connection requires both hardware and software to be installed to make the necessary links, at several levels.

Firstly, two or more computers each with a wireless network adapter installed and correctly configured complete the physical link. Secondly, the software components must be in place and configured on all computers to allow them to establish network communications, and finally the shared access to files and other resources must be enabled.

Installing a Wireless Network Adapter in Windows 98/2000/ME

In the next section we will install a wireless network adapter into a computer running Windows XP, but you may also have computers running pre-XP versions of Windows that you want to connect to your wireless home network. We'll deal with the installation of wireless network adapters under Windows 98/2000/ME in this section. The steps here describe the process for a laptop computer but the next section describes a desktop installation, so together these two sections will guide you through all possible combinations of operating system and computer type.

If your laptop is running Windows XP do not install the software drivers before installing the adapter hardware.

Under pre-XP versions of Windows, the configuration utility for your network adapter will ask you to specify the type of wireless network you will be connecting to. In this chapter we are looking at peer-to-peer or ad hoc connections, but you may also be installing your wireless adapter in order to connect to an Infrastructure mode network using a wireless access point or to connect to a hotspot. In this section we'll look at all these options.

If your laptop is running a pre-XP Windows version (98/2000/ME) and you plug the adapter in before installing the driver software, the New Hardware Wizard will install the device drivers but won't install the manufacturer's configuration utility.

Installing a laptop wireless network adapter in Windows 98/2000/ME

1 Before installing your laptop wireless network adapter card, switch on your laptop and insert the adapter manufacturer's setup CD into your CD-ROM drive

2 Click Start, Run and navigate to the setup utility on the installation CD. The file will be named Setup.exe or similar. Click OK

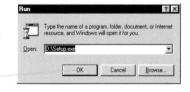

3 The manufacturer's setup utility will start. The details of the setup utility will vary depending on the manufacturer of your adapter, but the basic steps will be the same

4 Click Install to start the process

In this example, the configuration utility asks you to choose a network type – either Infrastructure mode or ad hoc mode.

Infrastructure mode will be the right choice if you are going to connect this computer to a network using an access point, which we will cover in chapter 5, or if you are going to connect to the Internet at a wireless hotspot, which we will cover in chapter 10.

5 If you are connecting to an access point or hotspot it will be in Infrastructure mode. Check this radio button

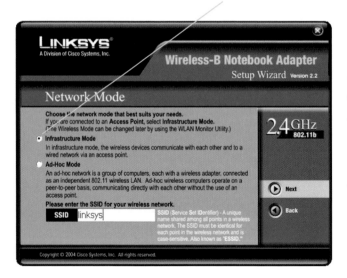

If you are connecting to a peer-to-peer network, check the ad hoc radio button

The Service Set ID (or SSID) is a unique name that you can choose to identify your wireless network. It is generally recommended that you change the default SSID to improve the security of your network. See step 6 on page 40.

If you are making an ad hoc connection you'll be able to enter the channel number to use. Start with channel 6, but be ready to try other channels if you experience interference. See chapter 11.

The channel number will be grayed out if you have selected infrastructure mode, because the adapter will sense the channel being used by the access point. See chapters 5 and 10.

6 If you know the SSID name of the ad hoc connection, access point or hotspot you are connecting to then enter it here. If not, you will always be able to update this when you make the connection

7 Confirm the settings you have selected if required

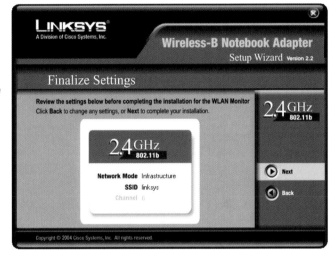

8 Power down the laptop and insert the wireless adapter card into the PC expansion slot in the side of your laptop

9 Restart your laptop. Windows will detect the new hardware and install the software drivers

You can insert the network adapter without powering down but it is not recommended. Some people go so far as to disconnect the power lead before inserting new hardware, but this is probably unnecessarily cautious.

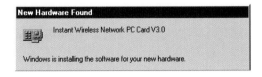

Windows may notify you of a version conflict if the installation process tries to overwrite a file with an older version. It is recommended to keep the newest version.

10 To complete the installation you will be asked to restart your computer

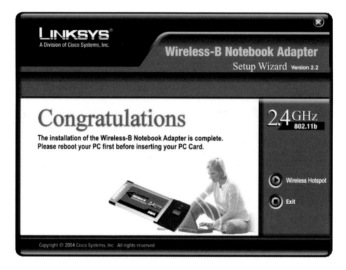

Since this is your first installation, you will not yet be within range of a wireless network, so your adapter will not yet be able to make a connection. We'll look at that in the following sections, after we go through the steps to install a wireless network adapter in a computer running Windows XP.

The next section also applies for a laptop running Windows XP.

Your wireless network adapter's setup wizard may include specific tools to set up hotspot access to the Internet, for example to T-Mobile or Boingo hotspots as in this example. We'll look at hotspots in chapter 10.

Installing a Wireless Network Adapter in Windows XP

In the last section we installed a wireless network adapter into a computer running pre-XP Windows 98/2000/ME.

If your second computer is also running an older version of Windows, follow the same steps for that computer. The following steps will apply if you are running Windows XP as the operating system on your second computer.

Installing the wireless adapter in Windows XP

Do not install the software drivers before installing the hardware if your computer is running Windows XP. You should only install the drivers first for computers that are running older versions of Windows such as 98/2000/ME.

1 Switch off your computer and install the wireless adapter, either by inserting it into a spare PCI slot, or by plugging it into a spare USB port, depending on the type of adapter you have bought

2 Switch on your computer and Windows will automatically detect the new hardware and start the New Hardware Wizard

3 Select "Install from a list or specific location" and click Next

4 Select "Search for the best driver in these locations" and "Include this location in the search"

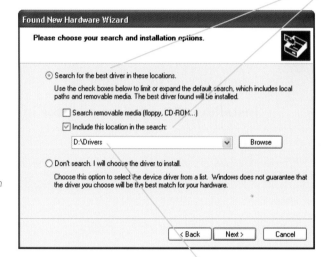

Use the Browse button to navigate your way to the installation CD in your CD-ROM drive.

5 Indicate the location of the device drivers on your installation CD and click Next

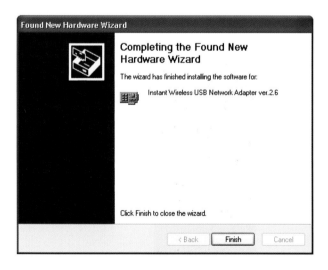

6 Click Finish. Your hardware is now installed. The next step is to make a wireless network connection to your other computer

Connecting to a Peer-to-Peer Wireless Network

Windows XP Zero Configuration will switch the wireless network adapter between ad hoc and infrastructure modes depending on the selected network.

After installing the network adapter hardware and software driver, the Windows XP Zero Configuration icon will appear in the notification area in the bottom right of your screen. To connect to an existing peer-to-peer (or ad hoc) network follow these steps. If you need to set up a new peer-to-peer connection in Windows XP, skip forward to the next section.

1 Start up one or more of the other computers in the peer-to-peer network and ensure that their wireless adapter cards are installed and operating correctly

Some older wireless network adapters may not support Windows XP Zero Configuration.

2 Right-click on the Windows XP Zero Configuration icon and select View Available Wireless Networks

3 Select the network you wish to connect to. Click Connect

WEP or Wired Equivalent Privacy is an aspect of wireless security that we will discuss in the final section of this chapter. See page 41.

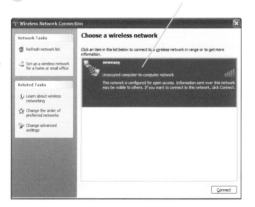

If WEP has not been enabled on the other computers, Windows XP will warn you that the network is unsecured

4 Click Connect Anyway to continue

If you have already made a wireless network connection and WEP is then changed from disabled to enabled on the other computers in the network, the properties for this connection will need to be manually reconfigured. This is described on page 41.

5 If WEP is enabled on the other computers in the network, enter the WEP Network key and click Connect

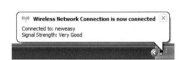

6 The Wireless Network Connection bubble will appear in the notification area once the connection is made

7 You can check the status of your wireless connection at any time by clicking on the Windows XP Zero Configuration icon

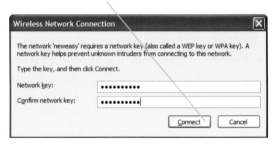

Wireless Network Connection status only shows the status of the physical link and does not show whether resources are accessible across the link. For example, if WEP is not correctly configured the status will still show as connected although you will not be able to reach shared resources. See Network Troubleshooting in chapter 11.

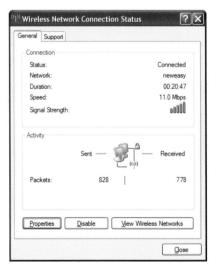

Signal strength and data speed are shown in the General tab

The Support tab gives information on the IP status of the connection

Creating a New Peer-to-Peer Wireless Network

The previous section showed you how to connect to a peer-to-peer network that had been set up on another computer. In this section you'll learn how to set up a new peer-to-peer wireless network connection using Windows XP.

1 Right-click the wireless connection icon and select Open Network Connections

2 Right-click on Wireless Network Connection and click Properties

3 In the Wireless Network Connection Properties dialog box select the Wireless Networks tab and click Advanced

4 Select "Computer-to-computer (ad hoc) networks only"

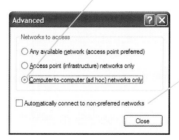

Uncheck "Automatically connect to non-preferred networks" and Close the dialog box

5 Under Preferred networks on the Wireless Network Connection Properties dialog box click Add

See page 32 for more on SSIDs.

The format of this dialog box will be different if you have not upgraded your Windows XP installation to SP2 (see page 120).

WEP or Wired Equivalent Privacy is a wireless security measure that we discuss in the next section.

An alphanumeric (or ASCII) Network key will only work with other Windows XP computers. In other cases you may need to use a hexadecimal format Network key (characters 0 to 9 and A to F).

If you are using WEP you will have to let other users know the Network key in order for them to connect.

6 Choose an SSID name for your new ad hoc network and enter it in the Wireless network properties dialog box

7 If you want to enable WEP, select WEP under Data encryption, choose a Network key for your network and enter it

8 Click OK and your new network connection will appear in the Preferred networks list. The red x on the icon indicates that no other computers are connected to the network

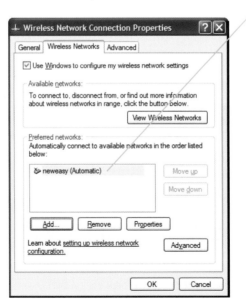

Other wireless enabled computers within range will now be able to see your ad hoc network and connect to it

Maintaining Security on Peer-to-Peer Wireless Networks

Even for a peer-to-peer network the transmitted wireless signal can propagate over distances of several hundred feet, depending on the type of location. For maximum security you should ensure that:

- WEP (Wired Equivalent Privacy) is enabled on all computers in the peer-to-peer network

If WEP is enabled on one computer but not on the other you will not be able to access shared files or other resources.

- Each network adapter is correctly configured using the same WEP key

If WEP is switched from disabled to enabled on a computer in a peer-to-peer network, the properties of the wireless network connection on the other computers will need to be updated in order to connect correctly.

Changing WEP status for an existing connection

1. Right-click the Windows XP Zero Configuration icon and click Status

2. In the Wireless Network Connection Status dialog box click Properties

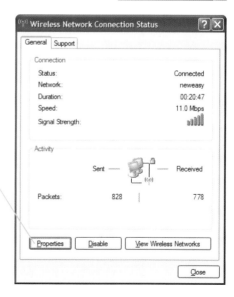

To change properties make sure you select from the Preferred networks list rather than the Available networks list.

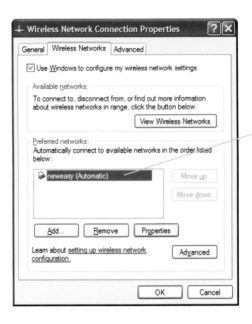

3 In the Properties dialog box, select the Wireless Networks tab

Select the connection you want to update from the Preferred networks list and click Properties

4 Under Data encryption select WEP from the drop down list

Of course, just as in your home, your privacy is only as good as the care you give to your keys. Using hard to guess keys and changing them regularly are important security steps that we'll cover in chapter 8.

Data sent over this connection will now be encrypted to ensure privacy

5 Click to uncheck "The key is provided for me automatically". You will be setting up WEP with a specific key that each computer will use to encrypt data

The Network key can be a 5 or 13 character alphanumeric string, or a 10 or 26 digit string of hexadecimal characters (1 to 9 and A to F).

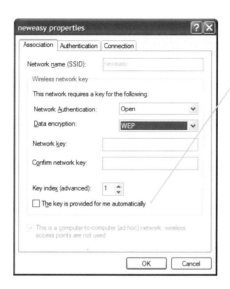

6 Choose a Network key and enter it. Confirm and click OK

Some wireless hardware uses a set of four keys from which one is selected using the Key index. Only change this value if you have set up other network hardware using a nonzero value for the key index.

7 Click View Wireless Networks

8 Windows XP will now show that the network connection is secured

9 Click Connect and you will be asked to enter the network key for the connection. Click Connect to make the connection

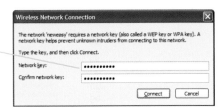

As well as enabling WEP, there are a number of other measures you should consider to establish and maintain the security of your wireless network connection. We will look at these when we discuss wireless security best practice in chapter 8.

Having created a peer-to-peer wireless connection between two or more computers, the next steps are to set up the software elements of the network connection under Windows XP and to enable resources such as folders and printers for sharing across the network. We will cover these steps in chapter 4.

Sharing Network Resources

Windows XP is designed to allow you to share a wide range of resources across your wireless home network – everything from pictures and music files to a printer, scanner or hard drive.

In this chapter you'll learn how to set up a network using Windows XP and then how to enable your resources for sharing with other computers on your network.

Covers

Network Setup Using Windows XP | 46

Sharing Files and Folders | 51

Sharing a Printer | 53

Sharing a Drive | 55

My Network Places | 58

Network Protocols and Services | 60

Internet Protocol Addressing | 62

Chapter Four

Network Setup Using Windows XP

Once your network adapter cards are installed and running in the computers that you want to network together, the Windows XP Network Setup Wizard will quickly take you through the steps to ensure that the necessary networking software components are installed and configured to enable the network connection.

1 Click Start, Settings, Network Connections or Start, Settings, Control Panel, Network Connections

If your folders are displayed in Classic mode, click Tools, Folder Options and "Show common tasks in folders" to make the Task Pane appear.

2 In the left hand Task Pane, select "Set up a home or small office network"

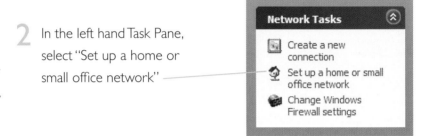

3 Click Next to start setting up the network connection

There's more on Internet connection sharing and Windows Firewall in chapter 6.

4 At each of the Wizard dialog boxes that follow make your choice and click Next

If you have unconnected network adapters, for example an unused dial-up modem, select "Ignore disconnected network hardware" when prompted.

A peer-to-peer network may not have an Internet connection, in which case select Other here and "This computer belongs to a network that does not have an Internet connection" in the following dialog box. Sharing your Internet connection is covered in more detail in chapter 6.

5 If the computer you are setting up connects to the Internet indicate how this is done

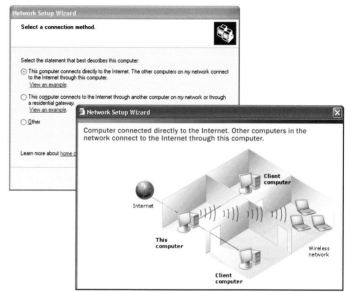

6 If the Wizard finds several connections on your computer you will be asked to select the one that connects to the Internet

If in doubt, read the information on the "Learn more" link.

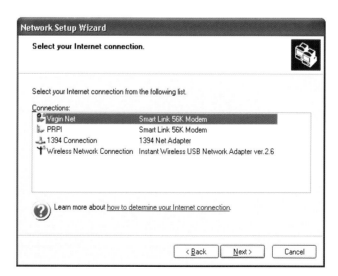

7 When several connections are found, the Wizard can determine for you which connections to use for linking to other computers, for example if your network has wired and wireless segments

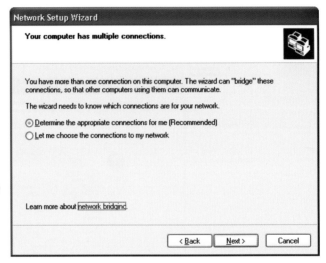

If your network has both wired and wireless links, network bridging will enable your wireless networked computers to access devices such as a DV camera linked to your main computer by Firewire (IEEE 1394). Follow the link to learn more about bridging.

8 Think of a description and name for your computer so that it can be uniquely identified in the network, and specify them

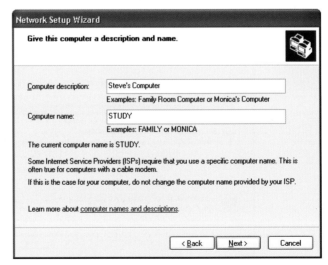

You can also change the computer or workgroup name by clicking Start, Settings, Control Panel, System, Computer Name, Change.

Computers in your network must all have different computer names but must all have the same workgroup name.

9 Think of a Workgroup name for your network, and specify it

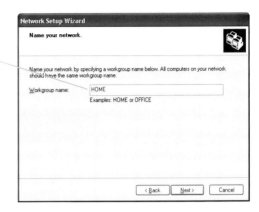

10 Select "Turn on file and printer sharing" to ensure that the Windows Firewall is configured to allow sharing on your network

Your settings will be different from those shown here.

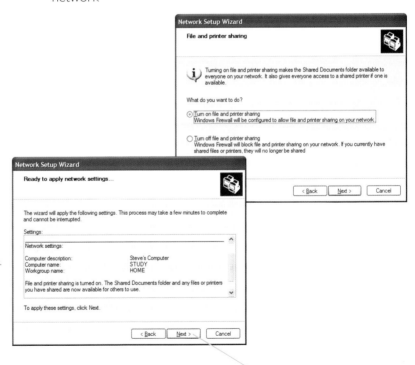

11 Make sure your settings are correct and then click Next. If any of the settings need to be changed, click Back until you reach the appropriate dialog box and make the necessary changes

12 Windows will then configure your computer for networking. Once that's completed, create a Network Setup Disk to configure the other computers you'll be using in your network

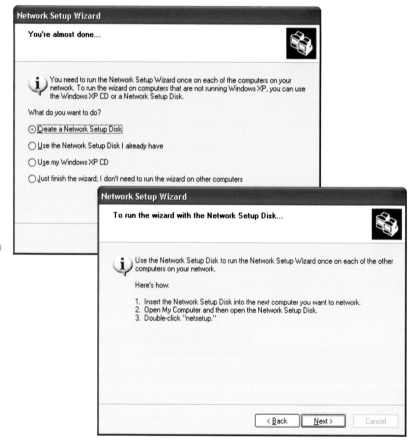

To run the netsetup program on your other computers navigate to the Setup Disk using My Computer and double-click on the netsetup application.

Remember the workgroup name must be the same for every computer in your network.

13 Click Finish and your first computer will be successfully set up for networking

14 Run the netsetup program from the Network Setup Disk on each of the other computers you'll be using in your network. When that's complete you'll be ready to start sharing resources between computers in your network

Sharing Files and Folders

Folders are the resources that you are likely to be sharing most often across your network. For a file to be shared it has to reside within a folder that has been set up for sharing.

Follow these steps to share a folder.

1 Right-click on the folder you wish to share and select Sharing and Security from the drop down menu

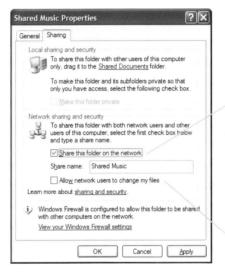

To be accessible to computers running earlier versions of Windows, the Share name should be at most 12 characters in length.

2 Select "Share this folder on the network". Choose a Share name by which the folder will be identified on the network, and enter it here. The Share name does not have to be the same as the original folder name

Allowing other users to change your files means they will be able to delete them as well. Don't check this box if you only want other users to be able to read the files in the shared folder.

3 If you want other users to be able to change your files as well as to read them, then check the "Allow network users to change my files" checkbox

4 The folder is now shared. The small hand that appears below the folder icon indicates that it is shared with other network users

Shared Music

Moving or renaming shared folders

If you try to move or rename a shared folder you will get a warning that the folder will no longer be shared after it has been renamed or moved.

Private folders

If the options on the Sharing tab are inactive, this is because the folder you are trying to share resides within another folder that has been designated as a private folder.

Move the folder you want to share out of the private folder or else change the parent folder so that it is no longer private.

You can prevent other network users from accessing a sub-folder within a shared folder by making the sub-folder private.

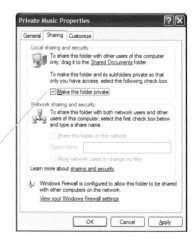

1 Right-click the sub-folder you want to protect, and select Security and Sharing

2 Select the "Make this folder private" check box and click Apply

Sharing a Printer

Sharing a printer with other users on your network is a two stage process. First the printer needs to be enabled for sharing on the computer that hosts the printer connection, and then the network printer needs to be set up on the other computers that want to print to it.

Enabling a printer for sharing

1. On the computer that the printer is connected to, access the printer by clicking Start, Control Panel, Printers and Faxes.

2. Right-click the printer that you want to share and click on Sharing...

Just as for shared folders, Network names longer than 12 characters may not be recognized by Windows versions earlier than XP.

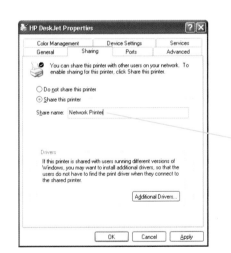

3. Select "Share this printer" and enter a Share name. This is the name that will identify the printer to all network users

If Windows XP does not have a suitable printer driver you will be asked to specify the location of the driver. You may need to find this from your printer manufacturer's website.

4. If any of the other computers that will use the shared printer are running older versions of Windows, Windows XP allows you to keep the printer drivers on the computer that maintains the shared printer. Click Advanced and indicate the additional drivers you need to install

5 A small hand appears below the printer icon to confirm that it is now available for sharing

HP DeskJet
0
Ready

Setting up a network printer

1 On each of the other networked computers in turn, click Start, Control Panel, Printers and Faxes, and select "Add a printer" from the Printer Tasks list

Printer Tasks
- Add a printer
- Set up faxing

2 The Add Printer Wizard will start. Click Next and on the next page select "A network printer". Click Next again

3 Select "Browse for a printer" and click Next

If the wizard only shows the workgroup but no printers, click on the workgroup icon to show computers, and then on the computer icon to show shared printers.

4 The wizard will identify other computers in the workgroup and list shared printers

5 Select the printer that you want to add and click Next. You will be asked whether you want this to be your default printer

Sharing a Drive

As well as sharing folders and printers, you can also share a complete drive, such as your hard drive, with other users on your network.

Although this might seem like an easy way to avoid having to set up sharing for a number of different folders, there is a risk in giving other users access to your main drive. A careless user could delete important system files and make your computer inoperable.

However, sharing a secondary drive, such as a CD-RW, may be useful if other computers on your network don't have this type of drive installed.

Enabling a drive for sharing

1   Click Start, My Computer and right-click the drive you want to share

2   Click "Sharing and Security..."

3   Click the "If you understand the risk but still want to share ..." link to continue to set up sharing for this drive

The Sharing options tab for a drive is identical to the one for a folder.

4 Select "Share this folder on the network", and enter a Share name

5 The familiar hand will appear beneath the drive icon to show that it is now shared on the network

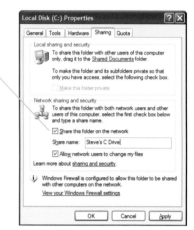

Local Disk (C:)

Mapping a shared drive

If you are going to access a shared drive frequently from another computer you can "map" the drive so that it appears in My Computer on the networked computer as if it was a local drive on that computer.

1 Open My Computer, right-click in the Toolbar and select Customize...

2 Select Map Drive from the list of buttons and click Add

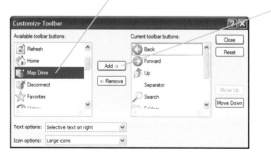

3 Select and Add the Disconnect toolbar button. Click Close

4 To map a network drive click the new Map Drive button on your My Computer toolbar

5 Select a drive letter from the drop down list of available unassigned letters and use the Browse button to locate the drive or folder that you want to map to that drive letter

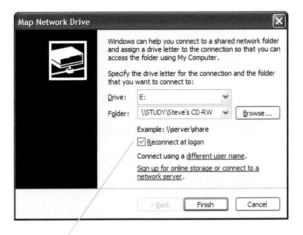

If the network connection cannot be established when you start up, Windows will warn you that it was unable to reconnect the mapped drive.

6 If you want Windows to connect to the drive each time you start up, select the "Reconnect at logon" check box. Click Finish

7 On the networked computer in My Computer the mapped drive will now appear alongside your local drive. The icon shows a cable beneath the drive to indicate that it is a network resource rather than a local drive

My Network Places

Now that your network is set up and a number of folders and devices have been enabled for sharing with other computers, you can use My Network Places to locate the shared resources and connect to information on the other computers.

If you will be using shared resources quite often it's useful to put a shortcut to My Network Places on your desktop.

Click Start, My Network Places, or if My Network Places does not appear in your Start Menu click Start, My Computer and then select My Network Places from the Other Places list in the Task pane

The computer that holds the shared folder or device must be switched on before you can access it. Windows will warn you if the computer is not accessible.

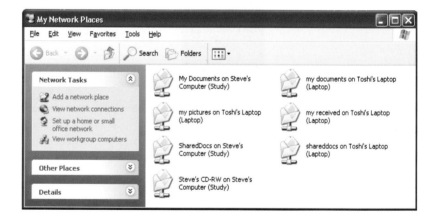

To access any shared network folder or device, double-click on the icon

The default view of My Network Places lists all shared resources alphabetically by name. You can also arrange the shared resources by computer or network location.

1 Right-click anywhere on the white space of the My Network Places window. A drop down menu will appear that gives you several options for arranging the shared resource icons

2 Identifying shared resources by their host computer is a useful option. Click Show in Groups and Arrange Icons By Computer to get this display

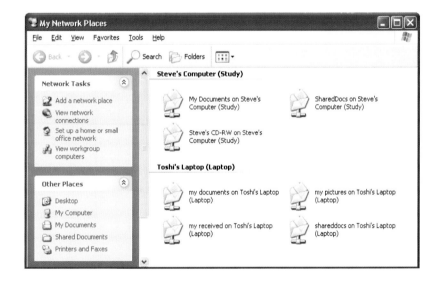

The last two sections of this chapter look at a couple of things that can occasionally come unstuck and cause a network connection to stop working.

Skip these for now if everything is working OK. Otherwise you may want to start here before referring to other troubleshooting steps in chapter 11.

Network Protocols and Services

Protocols and services are software components that your hardware needs to enable communication across your network connections. Windows XP will automatically install the protocols and services needed by your networking hardware. If any of these get accidentally deleted, follow these steps to reinstate them.

1 Click Start, Control Panel, Network Connections and right-click on the Network Connection you need to update

2 The protocols and services used by the connection are listed on the General tab as shown here

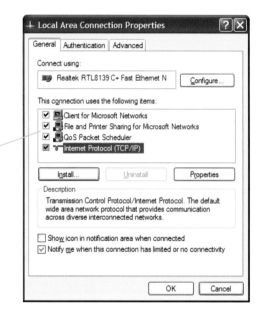

3 Your network connection, whether wired Ethernet or wireless, should have these four items listed: Client for Microsoft Networks, File and Printer Sharing for Microsoft Networks, QoS Packet Scheduler and Internet Protocol (TCP/IP)

If any of these items are missing the connection will not operate correctly.

4 If any of these items are missing click Install...

5 Select Client, Service or Protocol and click Add

Select Service if File and Printer Sharing or QoS was missing and Protocol if Internet Protocol was missing.

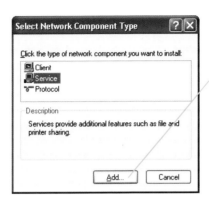

6 Select the item you wish to reinstall from the list of options provided

7 Click OK and the required Client, Service or Protocol will be installed

8 Depending on the item you are installing, you may be prompted to restart Windows XP before the change can become effective

Internet Protocol Addressing

Until the advent of Windows XP, setting up the Internet Protocol (IP) addresses of computers on the network was probably the most complex step in building a home network.

IP addresses are the heart of networking: it's these sequences of numbers that enable your computer to find a website on the other side of the world.

Windows XP handles IP address setup automatically for small networks, whether wireless or wired, but it's worthwhile knowing the basic steps in case things don't quite work as planned!

In IPv4, the current version of Internet Protocol, addresses are 32-bit binary numbers which are grouped into four 8-bit octets and represented as their decimal equivalents – numbers 0 to 255.

1 Open Network Connections (Click Start, Control Panel, Network Connections or your desktop shortcut)

2 Right-click on the Network Connection you need to update (Local Area Connection or Wireless Network Connection), and choose Properties from the short menu

3 On the General tab select Internet Protocol (TCP/IP) and click Properties

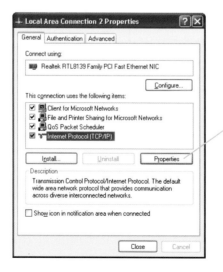

4 In the Internet Protocol Properties dialog box the default is "Obtain an IP address automatically". Don't change this setting unless given specific addresses by a Network Administrator

This default uses a Windows XP service that is called Automatic Private IP Address or APIPA.

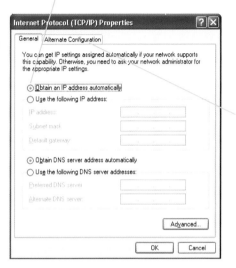

5 Select the Alternate Configuration tab

The Alternate Configuration tab is only available if automatic addressing is selected on the General tab.

6 If you have more than one network connection on this computer, this tab allows you to set an IP address for a connection where automatic address allocation is not available

Select "Automatic private IP address" (APIPA) if you are only connecting to one network

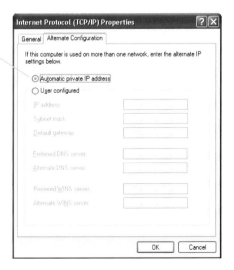

IP addresses run from 0.0.0.0 through to 255.255.255.255. Some ranges are reserved as private IP addresses to be used only in internal networks and not for communication through a router out into the Internet. In fact routers on the Internet will not forward data packets with source or destination addresses in these private ranges.

Computers with private IP addresses can still access the Internet using a process called Network Address Translation (NAT) provided by the router connecting your network to the Internet.

The reserved ranges for private IP addresses are:

- 10.0.0.0 through 10.255.255.255
- 172.16.0.0 through 172.31.255.255
- 192.168.0.0 through 192.168.255.255

If you need to specify private addresses for one of your network connections, choose one of these ranges and assign sequential addresses to all the computers in that segment of the network.

Specifying private IP addresses

This may be needed for example if you have a wireless network with IP addresses automatically assigned by a DHCP server in the access point, and one of your computers also has a simple wired Ethernet connection to another computer with no hub or switch.

1   Select "User configured"

2   Enter the IP address for the first computer in this private segment of your network. Click OK

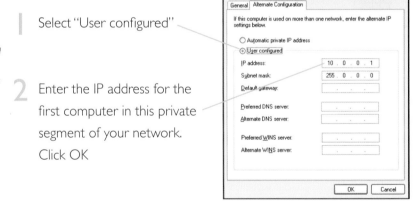

3   Repeat these steps for the other computer or computers on the segment of your network that requires private addressing. Use sequential IP addresses: the next computer you configure should be numbered 10.0.0.2, then 10.0.0.3 and so on. The Subnet mask should be unchanged and will be filled in automatically by Windows XP.

From Networking to Internetworking

In this chapter you'll learn about wireless networking using a central access point as a hub for wireless communication and as a gateway to the Internet. In contrast to the direct computer-to-computer or peer-to-peer setup we looked at in chapter 3, this type of network is called infrastructure mode.

We looked at choosing an access point for a wireless home network in chapter 2, so now we can get right on with installing and configuring the access point and setting up PCs for this type of network.

Covers

Introduction | 66

Setting up an Infrastructure Mode Wireless Home Network | 67

Locating Your Access Point | 68

Installing the Router and Configuring Network PCs | 69

Access Point / Router Configuration | 71

Additional Configuration Options | 77

Chapter Five

Introduction

As we noted in chapter 3, the IEEE 802.11b wireless networking standard supports two types of wireless connection between computers: peer-to-peer or ad hoc mode in which computers in the network communicate directly with each other, and infrastructure mode in which all communication is via a central access point.

The access point (AP) provides a link or bridge between a wired and a wireless network. The wired part of the network may be as simple as a connection to your broadband modem, or it may be a more extensive Ethernet network.

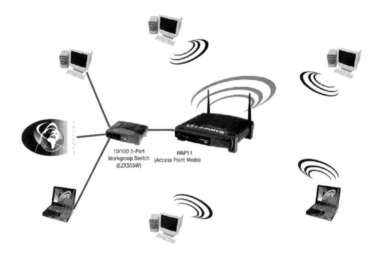

An AP may provide a number of functions in addition to giving wireless access into the wired network, such as:

Most of these functions are also provided by the host computer in a peer-to-peer wireless network with Windows XP running ICS and Windows Firewall (see chapter 6). An AP has the advantage that it does not tie up the host computer and it provides additional functions when it is combined with a switch/router.

- Internet connection sharing

- A server for allocating IP addresses

- A way of keeping internal IP addresses private

- Wireless access control and security

- Internet connection security and filtering (firewall)

- Network traffic switching and routing

Setting up an Infrastructure Mode Wireless Home Network

The steps you will need to follow to set up an infrastructure mode wireless network are a little more extensive than for the peer-to-peer connection, as there is one additional component – the access point – that needs to be installed and configured.

Drivers should be installed after installing hardware in Windows XP.

1 Install wireless network adapters into the computers in your network that you want to connect wirelessly to your access point. This was covered in chapter 3: see pages 31 to 36

2 If you have an always-on Internet connection, and you want computers to be able to access the Internet wirelessly when your main computer is not switched on, connect your cable or DSL modem up to your access point. See page 69

3 Connect up to your access point any other computers that you want to network using wired connections. See page 69

4 If you have a dial-up Internet connection and you want other computers in your network to access the Internet through your main computer, connect your access point just to this computer and not to the Internet connection

5 Configure your access point settings. See pages 71 to 76

6 Run the Windows Network Setup Wizard to configure the software components of your network. See page 46

7 Establish a wireless connection to the access point from each wireless enabled computer. To do this follow the same steps that we used when connecting to a peer-to-peer network. See page 37

Locating Your Access Point

If you are only expecting your wireless home network to cover a fairly small area within your home, perhaps one or two rooms, then it will not matter too much where you position your access point. You can choose the most convenient location, perhaps adjacent to your main PC or to your DSL or cable modem.

However, if you want as wide as possible an area to be covered you will need to consider a few things when deciding on the best location. Two things that will hurt your network performance are attenuation of the wireless signal and interference.

Loss of signal strength

If you have gone for classic Wi-Fi (the 802.11b variety) your network will be working using a radio signal that is actually very close to the signal inside the microwave — much the same frequency (a few GHz) only a lot weaker!

If you look in the front of a microwave oven (don't get too close if it's operating!) you'll see a fine metal mesh just inside the glass window. It's designed to reduce the amount of microwave radiation that gets through. This gives a good hint as to what's good and what's bad for your wireless network signal.

1. The worst thing for wireless signal loss is metal. Metal doors, floors, filing cabinets, even stud walls with an internal fire retardant foil, are all going to take a heavy toll on your signal strength – locate your access point as far away from them as possible

Of course, your signal is out in public air space if your AP is by a window. Don't forget the security measures covered in chapter 8.

2. Normal glass, on the other hand, is not a major problem. You can locate your AP by a window if you want to be able to pick up the signal outdoors

Interference

Microwave ovens and cordless phones are the biggest culprits in this department. There are a few things you can do:

1. The kitchen is not the obvious place to install your access point, but, just in case you do locate it there, remember that on top of the microwave oven is certainly not the best spot!

We'll look further into making the most of your signal strength in chapter 9.

2. Cordless phones also operate on the same wireless frequency as Wi-Fi. Don't set your access point up right beside your cordless phone base station or your data throughput will suffer.

Installing the Router and Configuring Network PCs

If you have chosen a simple access point rather than a combined access point/router for your wireless home network, you can disregard the steps that refer to wired connections to the device.

An access point/router will manage Internet traffic from your wireless home network to your broadband Internet connection. After wiring the access point/router into your network your PCs' configurations will need to be checked to make sure they are set up to work with the router.

Connecting the access point/router to your network

1 Power down all your hardware before you start wiring up

2 If you have PCs you want to network with wires, connect an Ethernet network cable from the Ethernet port of each one to any of the ports on the back of your access point/router

Make sure you connect your modem and router through the correct port. It may be labeled WAN or Internet.

3 Connect another Ethernet cable between your broadband Internet modem and the WAN or Internet port on the back of the access point/router

4 Power up your network hardware. The router's front panel LED corresponding to the port connected to your PC should light up, indicating that the Ethernet link is active

Configuring your PCs

Each PC needs to be configured to obtain an IP address from the access point/router and must also have the TCP/IP protocol installed and available for use. Check this as follows:

If your Control Panel is in Category view, click "Switch to Classic View" in the task panel.

1 Open Network Connections either from your desktop icon or from Start, Control Panel, Network Connections

2 Double-click the Local Area Network connection and click Properties

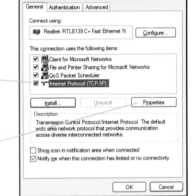

3 On the General tab, verify that the Internet Protocol (TCP/IP) box is checked

If TCP/IP is not checked, follow the steps on page 60 to install this protocol.

4 Select Internet Protocol and click Properties

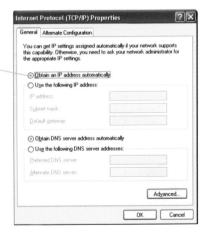

5 On the General tab, verify that the "Obtain an IP address automatically" radio button is selected

6 Click OK

If you have not yet run the Network Setup Wizard you will need to do so now (see page 46).

The same settings will need to be checked on all the PCs in the network, including those that will be using wireless links to the access point/router.

Access Point / Router Configuration

To get your access point/router up and running you will need to update some basic settings that configure your Internet access and your wireless mode. More advanced options will be covered in the next section.

1   Your access point/router will probably have a web based configuration utility. Start a web browser on one of the PCs on your network. Enter the AP's IP address in the address field of the browser. You'll find the IP address in your user documentation

Some APs have a configuration port, usually a USB port, as an alternative to using a web based utility.

2   Changing configuration settings will require you to enter an administration password. Check your manufacturer's documentation and enter the required default password

You should change the default password to ensure security of your network. See page 74.

3   The initial setup screen for your configuration utility will be displayed in the browser window

The specific layout of the setup utility for your hardware may differ from the one shown, but the basic settings you will have to update will be very similar.

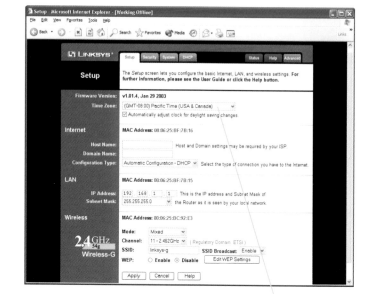

4   The first configuration step is to select your time zone and enable automatic clock changes.

5 If required by your Internet Service Provider (ISP), enter the Host Name and Domain Name

The MAC address shown here is the address of the port to which your Internet cable is connected.

Internet

MAC Address: 00:06:25:BF:7B:16

Host Name:		Host and Domain settings may be required by your ISP.
Domain Name:		
Configuration Type:	Automatic Configuration - DHCP ∨	Select the type of connection you have to the Internet.

6 Select the Internet configuration type for your Internet connection from the drop down menu

7 If your ISP connection does not use DHCP, you will be asked to provide additional information:

This information will be provided to you by your ISP.

For **Static IP** you'll need the IP address, Subnet mask, Default Gateway and a Domain Name Server (DNS) IP address

Configuration Type:	Static IP ∨	Select the type of connection you have to the Internet.
Internet IP Address:	0 . 0 . 0 . 0	
Subnet Mask:	0 . 0 . 0 . 0	
Gateway:	0 . 0 . 0 . 0	
DNS (Required):	1: 0 . 0 . 0 . 0	
	2: 0 . 0 . 0 . 0	
	3: 0 . 0 . 0 . 0	

PPPoE is used sometimes by DSL-based ISPs. The information you need to enter can be obtained from your ISP.

For **PPPoE** you'll need your User Name and Password

Configuration Type:	PPPoE ∨	Select the type of connection you have to the Internet.
User Name:		
Password:		
○ Connect on Demand: Max Idle Time 5 **Min.**		
⊙ Keep Alive: Redial Period 30 **Sec.**		

PPTP is only used in Europe.

For **PPTP** you'll need an IP address, Subnet Mask, default Gateway, User Name and Password

Configuration Type:	PPTP ▼	Select the type of connection you have to the Internet.

Internet IP Address:	0 . 0 . 0 . 0	
Subnet Mask:	0 . 0 . 0 . 0	
Gateway:	0 . 0 . 0 . 0	
User Name:		
Password:		
○ Connect on Demand: Max Idle Time	5	Min.
⊙ Keep Alive: Redial Period	30	Sec.

8 Lastly, configure the access point's wireless settings. If you have an 802.11g AP, Mixed mode will allow your network to operate with both 802.11g and 802.11b equipped computers

Wireless	MAC Address: 00:06:25:BC:92:E3
2.4 GHz 54g Wireless-G	Mode: Mixed ▼
	Channel: 11 - 2.462GHz ▼ (Regulatory Domain: ETSI)
	SSID: linksys-g SSID Broadcast: Enable ▼
	WEP: ○ Enable ⊙ Disable Edit WEP Settings

Don't forget to change the SSID from its default value (see page 40). This and disabling the SSID broadcast are recommended security practices.

You can select the wireless channel and SSID, just as we saw when setting up a peer-to-peer connection. An additional feature in infrastructure mode is that you can disable the SSID broadcast

The passphrase option is generally specific to a particular manufacturer. You will need to manually enter the resulting keys if your wireless adapters are from different manufacturers.

WEP should be set up just as for a peer-to-peer network. See page 41.

If you haven't done so you will also need to run the Windows Network Setup Wizard (see page 46).

Additional settings

With the basic settings of your access point/router setup as described in the last few sections, your infrastructure mode wireless network will be up and running, and your networked computers will be able to connect to the Internet through the router.

Your AP/router will have a range of additional functions including security and network management. In this section we'll take a look at some of these features.

Security

We'll cover the full range of security issues in chapter 8.

1 On the Security tab you will be able to set an administration password for the configuration utility. Change the default password to prevent unauthorized access to your network settings

2 Most routers support VPN passthrough, which is used to allow secure access from the Internet into the network

3 You may want to enable one PC on your network to operate as a DMZ host if you want to host websites or Internet games

General settings

A general settings or System tab will allow you to control some of the general features of your AP/router.

If things get in a mess you can always reset the factory defaults and get safely back to square one!

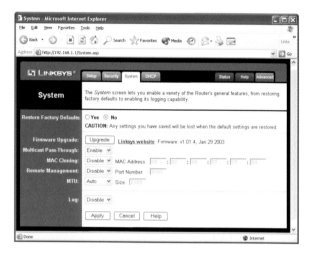

MAC address cloning

MAC address cloning allows you to replace the MAC address of the router with another MAC address. Some ISPs require you to register the MAC address of your computer and this feature allows your router to use this registered MAC address. If you need to use this feature follow these steps:

1 Find your computer's MAC address by typing "ipconfig /all" at the DOS command prompt (see page 171). The MAC address is the 12-digit "physical address" of the network adapter that is used for your Internet connection

2 Select Enable from the drop down menu beside the MAC Cloning option. The MAC address input field will now become active

3 Enter the 12-digit MAC address of your network adapter into the field provided

4 Click Apply to enable the revised settings

Multicast pass through

Multicast pass through allows an incoming data packet to be forwarded to multiple computers within your network. Keep the default if you want to enable this feature.

Enabling remote management will allow anyone who knows the IP address and password to change your router settings via the Internet.

Remote management

Remote management will allow you to change your router settings via the Internet. You will need to know your router's IP address and password in order to log on and change your settings.

Router log

A Log feature will keep track of all traffic on your Internet connection. Typically a log will be kept of all incoming Internet traffic showing the source IP address and the destination port number, as well as all outgoing traffic showing the originating IP address within your network and the destination URL or IP address.

If your router does not have this feature you can also activate a log using the Windows Firewall, which we will cover in the next chapter.

MTU

MTU is the Maximum Transmission Unit – the largest data packet size that is permitted for Internet transmission. You should not need to change this.

See page 124 for firmware upgrades to network adapters.

Firmware upgrades

Firmware, as you might expect, is half way between software and hardware! It refers to the software held in memory inside a hardware device that controls the operation of the device.

If you upgrade firmware you may find that the device's settings are reset to factory defaults. Make a note of your settings before upgrading!

Many devices such as network adapters, access points and routers allow firmware to be upgraded automatically over the Internet. This will enable you to take advantage of any bug fixes or new features that have been added to your hardware device.

Additional Configuration Options

In addition to the basic access point and router configuration options covered in the last section, most APs provide a wide range of additional configurable options.

The functions covered in this section need not concern you in your early days of wireless networking, but you may need to come back to this section as your networking skills and requirements become more sophisticated.

Assigning addresses in your network

Many routers can provide Dynamic Host Configuration Protocol (DHCP) server functions, which assign IP addresses to computers in your network automatically.

Although using DHCP is the easy option, manually assigning IP addresses gives an extra level of security in a wireless network.

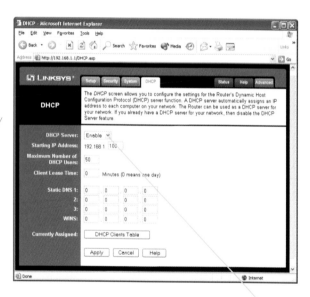

Make sure you only have one DHCP server enabled in your network!

To use the router's DHCP server click Enable. The default setting will generally not need to be changed

Ensure that all PCs in your network are configured to obtain an IP address automatically (see page 63)

An option on this tab will allow you to view a list of IP addresses currently assigned by the DHCP server

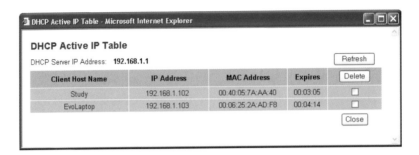

Controlling access using Media Access Control

Most of the advanced wireless settings can be left at their default values, but one option you may wish to use is Media Access Control, or MAC filtering. Every network adapter has a unique MAC address that can be used to permit or deny access.

Select Enable from the drop down menu against MAC filtering

Select whether you want the access point to permit or prevent access for the MAC addresses in the filter list

Enter the permitted or excluded MAC addresses in the filter list

You'll need to ask each of your allowed users to find the MAC address of their wireless adapter using the ipconfig /all command at the DOS prompt. See page 171.

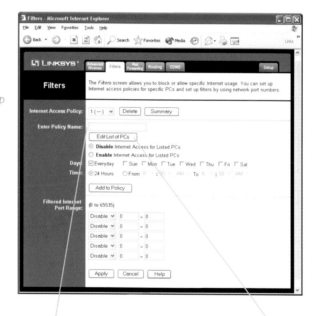

Internet filters

Most routers provide a range of filters that can be configured to block or enable particular kinds of Internet access.

For this router, up to ten different access policies can be defined, each for a specified list of PCs.

If you are using DHCP in your network you will have to identify PCs by their MAC addresses.

Enter a name for the access policy and list PCs to which this policy applies

2   Specify the filters to be applied to this policy. Filtering on website URL, keyword, access time or day of the week are typical options available

3   Click Summary to see an overview of your access policies

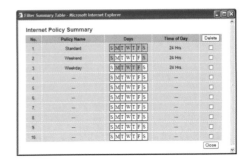

Port forwarding

You will need to configure this advanced option if any computer on your network is going to be acting as a web server, email server or FTP server. Port Forwarding ensures that requests for these services are forwarded to the correct computer on your network.

   For each application requiring access through an external port you will need to enter the port range being used

Information on the port ranges used will be in your application documentation.

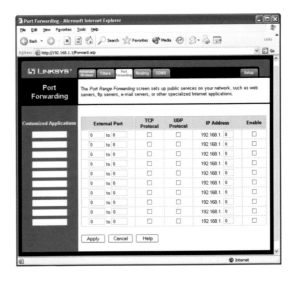

Any computer that is having a port forwarded must have a static IP address. Disable DHCP, navigate to the TCP/IP Properties, General tab (see page 63) and enter the static IP address there after clicking "use the following IP address".

Routing is an advanced configuration option that you will not have to worry about unless you are building a complex network.

The table is known, not too surprisingly, as the routing table.

2 Indicate which protocols are to be forwarded

3 Enter the static IP address of the computer that is serving this application

The documentation for your particular server application will give you further information on any specific requirements for that application.

Routing

Routing is one of many little pieces of technological magic that make the Internet work. When you enter a website name into your browser, for example www.ineasysteps.com, one of the first things that happens is that your browser finds a path out into the Internet to get the website name translated into the IP address of the computer that serves up the web page that you're after.

Then, once the IP address is known, your request is sent out to that hosting computer, the server, and it gets received and actioned. The process of marshalling, or routing, messages around the Internet is controlled by devices called routers.

Every router holds a table of IP addresses of other routers that can help it find the route to another computer. No single router knows about the whole of the Internet – each knows just a little about its own local neighborhood – but by working together they keep the whole thing moving.

The routing functions of your hardware can be used in two modes, either as a gateway to the Internet or as a router within a more complex network with other routers. For most home applications you will be using the gateway option.

Router setup

1 Select the appropriate operating mode for your network: router or gateway

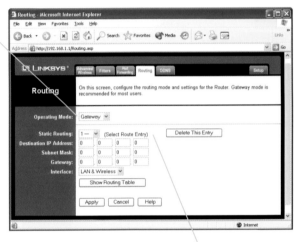

2 You will have the option to build a static routing table to specify routing paths for network traffic. Only do this if you are skilled at network configuration

With Dynamic Routing, a router will share its routing tables with others in response to RIP (Router Information Protocol) messages.

3 Router mode will also include an option to use dynamic routing (RIP) which allows the router to build its own routing table

RIP will only be needed on the LAN/Wireless side if you have a very complex network.

4 Specify whether RIP is to be enabled on the WAN side of the router, the LAN/Wireless side or both

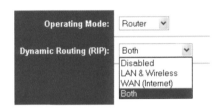

In most cases your router will be configured in the factory default operating mode as a gateway to the Internet.

In this case its router table will be very short as it only needs to know one other IP address – that of your Internet service provider.

Internet Connections and Firewalls

In this chapter we look at sharing an Internet connection among the computers in your wireless home network. You'll learn how to manage the Internet connection from a network computer and how to use the Windows Firewall.

We'll see how to enable and use the Windows Firewall log file to monitor Internet traffic. Finally we'll see how you can log on to your home network remotely.

Chapter Six

Covers

Internet Connection Sharing | 84

Managing a Shared Internet Connection | 86

Using Windows Firewall | 88

Remote Access to Your Wireless Home Network | 93

Internet Connection Sharing

The host computer must be switched on for other computers to be able to use its Internet connection.

Internet Connection Sharing (ICS) in Windows XP allows you to configure one computer in your network as a host through which all other workgroup computers can connect to the Internet.

If you have an always-on connection, you can also connect your access point/router directly to your Internet modem (page 69), in which case you will not need to use ICS.

Changing ICS Host Settings

1   To access ICS settings, open Network Connections from your Desktop or from the Start menu on the computer that hosts your Internet connection and right-click the Shared Internet Connection icon

2   Choose Properties... and in the Properties dialog box click Advanced

Windows Firewall settings can also be changed on the Advanced tab. Windows Firewall is covered in the next section.

3 Check "Allow other network users to connect ..." to enable ICS

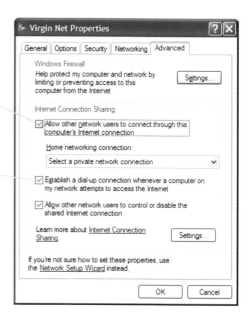

4 Check "Establish a dial-up connection ..." if you want Windows XP to make the connection when a workgroup computer accesses the Internet

This option only appears if you are sharing a dial-up connection.

5 Select the home network Internet connection that you want to share from the drop down list

If the check box is cleared other computers will only be able to access the Internet when the host computer has opened the connection.

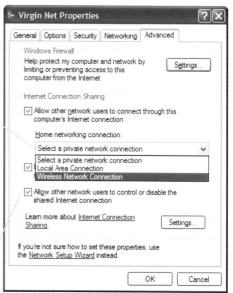

6 If you check the box to "Allow other network users to control or disable the shared Internet connection", each workgroup computer will be able to control the shared connection as if it was the host

Managing a Shared Internet Connection

If you have allowed other network users to control or disable the shared Internet connection, then even if these users do not have direct access to the host computer they will still be able to view connection statistics, monitor the status of the connection and connect to or disconnect from your ISP.

Connecting to the Internet using ICS

1 Open Network Connections from your Desktop or from the Start menu. If network computers' control of the dial-up connection is enabled you will see a group called Internet Gateway in the folder

2 Right-click the icon for your Internet connection and select Connect from the drop down menu

3 Windows XP will open the shared Internet connection and let you know that it is trying to connect

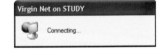

4 When the connection is made, a bubble will appear above the notification area

5 In the Network Connections folder the Internet Gateway will now be shown as Connected

Viewing Internet connection status

If you have more than one connection active, each connection will be identified as you roll the mouse over each icon in the notification area.

1 Right-click on the icon for the shared Internet connection in the notification area and select Status

2 You will be able to check your connection speed and how many data packets have been sent and received through the gateway to the Internet

Disconnecting a shared Internet connection

1 Right-click on the icon for the shared Internet connection in Network Connections and select Disconnect, or click Disconnect in the Status dialog box above

If you have trouble disconnecting the Internet connection from the network computer, you can always disconnect at the host computer.

In Network Connections the Internet Gateway will now be shown as Disconnected

Using Windows Firewall

If you are using a residential gateway or access point to connect to the Internet, the firewall product that comes with your gateway is an alternative to using Windows Firewall.

Once you have established a connection to the Internet from your network you should consider using the Windows Firewall to prevent unwanted access to your computer from the Internet.

Windows Firewall works by keeping track of the IP addresses of Internet sites that you are connecting to and only accepting incoming data packets that originated from a recognized IP address.

Enabling Windows Firewall

1 Open Network Connections from your Desktop or click Start, Connect To, Show all connections

If your network has more than one Internet connection you need to enable Windows Firewall on each connection.

2 Right-click on the Internet connection you want to protect, and select Properties...

3 Select the Advanced tab and click Settings...

4 Select On to enable Windows Firewall on this connection

Enabling the Windows Firewall Log File

When Windows Firewall is activated, you can configure the firewall to keep a record of events such as dropped packets or successful connections. You can then view the log file to see what activity has taken place across the firewall.

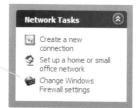

1 Open Network Connections and click on "Change Windows Firewall settings" in the Network Tasks panel

2 Under Security Logging click Settings...

3 In the Log Settings dialog box, select the events that you want to log: "Log dropped packets", "Log successful connections" or both

4 Change the log file name or location if you want to store it somewhere other than in the default location, and click OK

5 You can change the size limit of the log file up to 32 MB. When the file reaches its maximum size the contents are written to a file called pfirewall.log.1 and new data is collected in pfirewall.log

You occasionally will need to do some housekeeping and delete old log files!

Viewing the Windows Firewall Log File

When Windows Firewall is activated, you can view the log file by opening it with a text editor such as Notepad. The log file contains information about dropped packets or successful connections in time order.

1 Open Notepad by clicking Start, All Programs, Accessories, Notepad

If you chose a filename or directory other than the default, look there for the log file.

2 Open the log file in Notepad by clicking File, Open, My Computer, Local Drive (C:), WINDOWS, pfirewall.log

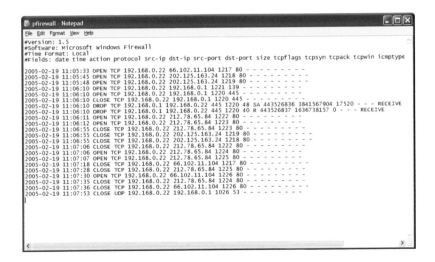

After the header information, each line in the log file records an action on an incoming or outgoing data packet. The first six fields record:

- Date and Time

- Action: such as opening or closing a connection or dropping a packet

- Protocol: mostly TCP

- Source IP address: the address of the computer that initiated the communication

- Destination IP address: the address of the computer that received the communication

If your have connected your Internet modem directly to your wireless access point/router, you will be able to use the router log instead of the Windows Firewall log to monitor traffic (see page 76).

Using the Firewall Log File to monitor Internet traffic

The information saved in the log file can be used to monitor which websites have been accessed over the protected Internet connection. Each log entry where the action was Open records a request from a user to open a connection to the website indicated by the destination address. To identify the site follow these steps:

Open the log file in Notepad by clicking File, Open, My Computer, Local Drive (C:), WINDOWS, pfirewall.log

For the Open connection that you want to trace, double-click the destination IP address (the second of the two IP addresses on the line), then right-click and select Copy

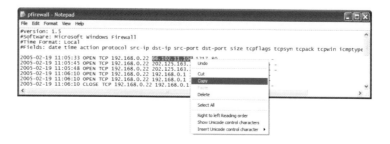

3 Start a web browser. Paste the address into the Address field in your browser and click Go

4 The browser will open a connection to the IP address and the web page will appear

Remote Access to Your Wireless Home Network

If you need to access files on your wireless home network while at work or traveling, Windows XP allows you to set up a connection that you can use to dial in to your home network from a remote location.

This is achieved by setting up a dial-up connection so that one computer on your network can act as a remote access server.

Accessing your home network remotely

If you are in Windows classic folder view, start the New Connection Wizard by clicking File, New Connection...

1 Connect the dial-up modem of the computer that will act as the remote access server to the phone line

2 On the computer that will act as the remote access server, click Start, Connect to, Show all connections

3 Click "Create a new connection" in the Network Tasks panel, and click Next on the New Connection Wizard's opening screen

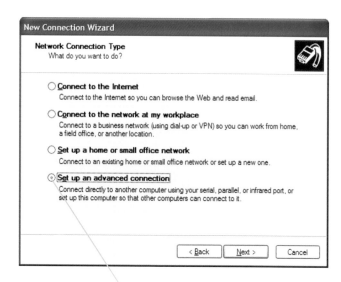

4 Click "Set up an advanced connection" and click Next

5 Click "Accept incoming connections" in the Advanced Connection Options dialog box, and click Next

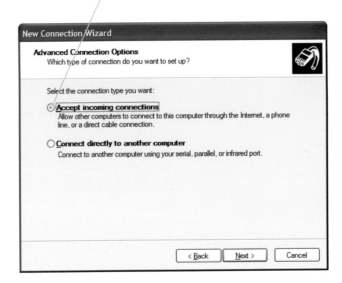

6 In the Devices for Incoming Connections dialog box, select the check box beside each device you want to use for incoming connections

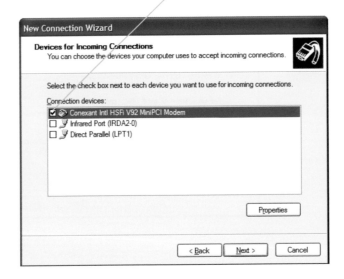

If you want to find out more about VPNs check out some of the information websites in chapter 12.

7 Click "Do not allow virtual private connections" in the following dialog box

8 In the User Permissions dialog box, select the user accounts that you want to be accessible from the incoming connection. Then click Next

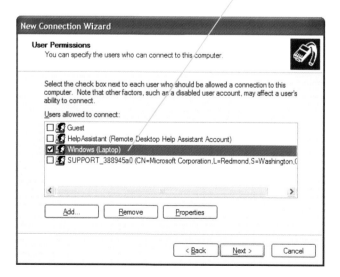

9   In the Networking Software dialog box, make sure that File and Printer Sharing for Microsoft Networks is enabled if you want incoming connections to have full access to shared network resources

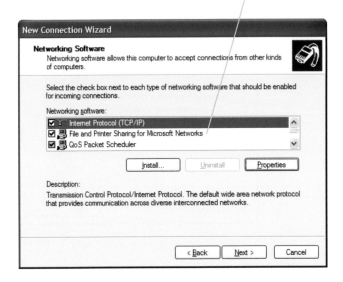

10   Click Next and click Finish to complete the new connection

Your remote access serving computer will need to be switched on in order for you to be able to access it remotely.

To connect to your computer simply use a dial-up connection on your workplace computer or laptop when traveling. Dial in to the number of the phone line connected to the computer you have set up as your remote access server and log on to that computer in the usual way.

If the computer you are dialing in to may be in use by another user, then it is best to have Fast User Switching enabled on that computer since this ensures that the other user has the opportunity to close their session properly before you log on.

Access the Help and Support Center from the Start menu.

Check out the Microsoft Help and Support Center to find out about enabling Fast User Switching.

Seven

Managing Your Wireless Network

In this chapter we look at tools to help you manage your wireless home network. Following these steps will ensure that you get maximum performance from your network, that it is secure and that you are not risking loss of important data shared across your network.

Covers

Monitoring Network Performance | 98

Backing Up Your Network Data | 101

Running the Windows XP Backup Utility | 103

Advanced Backup Options | 106

Completing the Backup | 108

Restoring Backed Up Network Data | 109

Advanced Restore Options | 111

Completing the Restore | 112

Monitoring Network Performance

Windows XP provides a set of tools to allow you to monitor the throughput and speed performance of your network. You may want to use these tools if you find that data transfer between parts of your network is slow and you suspect there are bottlenecks.

Network performance using Windows Task Manager

You can also start Task Manager by pressing Ctrl + Alt + Del

1 Start Windows Task Manager by right-clicking in the Task Bar and selecting Task Manager

2 Select the Networking tab on the Windows Task Manager dialog box

If you only have one active network connection then the tab will only display one graph.

3 The Networking tab shows you real-time information about the usage of each of the active network adapters on your computer

Running Windows Task Manager on the computer that hosts a shared Internet connection can be useful to see whether large files are being downloaded elsewhere in the network. This may affect performance.

4 You can change the update speed of the graph by clicking View, Update Speed, or you can select to view bytes sent and received as well as total traffic by clicking View, Network Adapter History and selecting the information you want to show on the graph

5 The data displayed below the network performance graphs can also be customized by clicking View, Select Columns...

6 Select the data items that you wish to monitor from the list and click OK

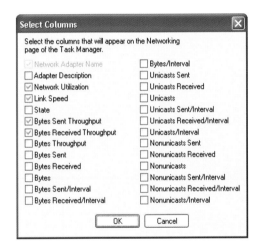

Managing Performance

Windows XP includes an advanced performance management tool called Performance.

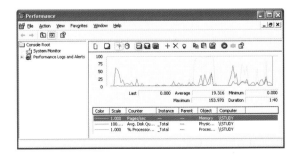

To start Performance click Start, Control panel, Administrative Tools, Performance.

2 To select the items you want to monitor, check that System Monitor is selected in the left-hand pane and click the New Counter Set button. Click the Add button

Roll your mouse over the other toolbar buttons to check out some additional features of the Performance tool.

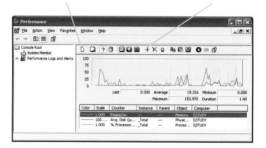

3 In the Add Counters dialog box, select Network Interface from the drop down list of Performance objects

4 Select the network adapter you want to monitor from the list of instances

5 Select the data you want to monitor and click the Add button to include each item in the performance chart. Click Close to complete your selection

You can also use Performance to create a log file of data for later viewing, or to send a notification when a performance measure moves outside a preset range.

6 The chart will display the performance items you have selected

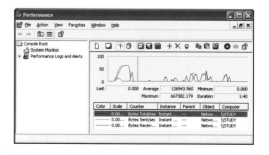

Backing Up Your Network Data

Although Windows XP does have a utility to back up files, it is not included in the default installation unless you are running Windows XP Professional. In Windows XP Home, you will first have to locate and install the utility before you can back up files.

This is well worth a little digging around if you want to reduce the risk of losing data as a result of accidental deletion, viruses, hardware problems or other gremlins.

Installing the Backup utility in Windows XP Home

Locate your Windows XP CD and insert it into your CD drive. The CD will start automatically and the Windows XP Welcome page will open

If the CD does not run automatically, double-click the CD icon under My Computer.

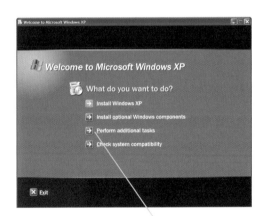

Click "Perform additional tasks", and then "Browse this CD"

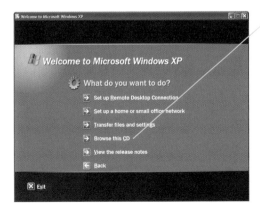

3 Double-click the VALUEADD folder

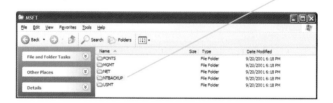

4 Double-click the MSFT folder and then the NTBACKUP folder

5 Double-click the NTBACKUP program installation file

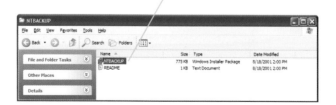

6 The Windows XP Backup utility will be installed on your computer

7 The Backup utility will appear under Start, All Programs, Accessories, System Tools

Running the Windows XP Backup Utility

1 Click Start, All Programs, Accessories, System Tools, Backup. The Backup utility will load and start by looking for backup devices

2 The Backup or Restore Wizard will open. Click Next

3 To back up, select the "Back up files and settings" radio button

4 Alternatively, if you are ready to restore a previous backup, select the "Restore files and settings" button. Click Next

5 Select the items you wish to back up. Click Next

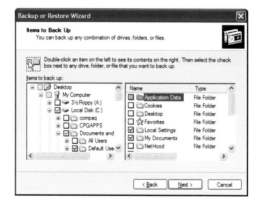

6 If you select "Let me choose what to back up", you will be able to select individual folders and files from anywhere on your computer to add to your backup set. Click Next

7 Whether you have selected one of the first three options at Step 5, or chosen the specific files and folders to back up in Step 6, you will now be asked to select the device you wish to back up to. Select the device from the drop down list or use Browse to navigate to the folder where you want to save your backup file

If you decide to back up to a CD-RW, you will not be able to select that device directly. You need to choose a set of files to back up that is no larger than the capacity of your CD, and back that set up to a file. Once the file is complete you can copy it to the CD-RW.

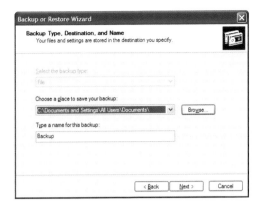

8   Once you have identified the backup destination click Next

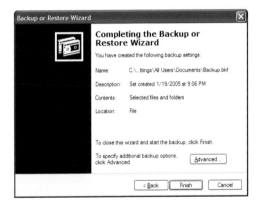

9   Review the settings you have selected. Click Back if you need to change your settings or Finish to continue with the backup. Click Advanced here if you wish to select the type of backup to perform

Advanced backup options are covered in the next section.

Advanced Backup Options

On the first Advanced page, five options are available from the drop down list:

- Normal: backs up the selected files and marks each file as backed up

- Copy: backs up selected files but does not mark as backed up

- Incremental: only backs up selected files if they were created or modified since the previous backup; marks each file as backed up

- Differential: like Incremental but does not mark the files as backed up

- Daily: backs up only files created or modified today

1   Select the type of backup you wish to create and click Next

2   This Advanced option screen allows you to select verification and hardware compression and to enable shadow volume copying

Select the options you want to use in completing your backup and click Next

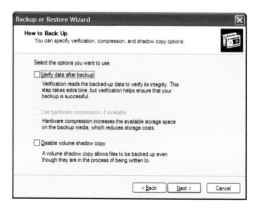

Verification may double the time taken for your backup. Shadow volume copying will only be necessary if you are backing up files that other users on your network are using at the same time.

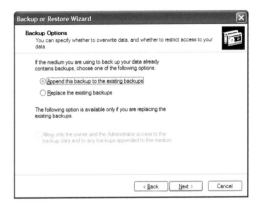

3 The next Advanced option allows you to either overwrite existing backups or append this new backup to existing backups. Select your preferred option and click Next

Set Schedule will allow you to set up routine backups and to control various settings for the backup jobs – such as not starting the backup job if the computer is running on batteries.

4 The final Advanced backup option allows you to specify when you want your backup to take place. Select your preferred timing and click Next

5 The Backup Wizard completion page will once again allow you to review your settings and go back to make any changes that may be necessary. Click Finish to end the wizard. If you have chosen to do your backup Now, the backup will start

Completing the Backup

1 The Backup utility will start by determining the size of the backup that has been specified

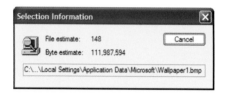

2 The Backup utility will then start to create the backup file in the location specified

3 When the process is complete a short summary of the backup will be displayed. To see more details click Report...

Restoring Backed Up Network Data

Restoring backup files and folders is a simple reverse of the original backup operation. You will be able to restore individual files, folders or complete backups, either to their original location or to specified alternative locations.

Restoring backup data

1   To restore previously backed up files, start the Backup by clicking Start, All Programs, Accessories, System Tools, Backup. Select "Restore files and settings". Click Next

2   A list of previous backups will be displayed. Select the backup file that you want to restore files from

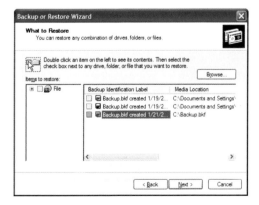

3 Navigate to the folders and files that you wish to restore. You can select anything from a single file or folder to the full backup. Click Next

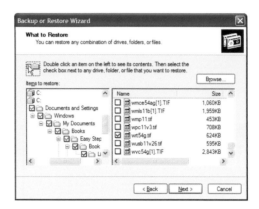

4 The Restore Wizard completion page will allow you to review the options selected. Click Back to change your selection or Next to proceed with the restore

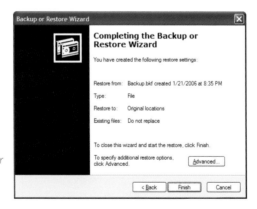

If you select other than the original location the next screen will prompt for the destination.

5 Click Advanced... for advanced restore options

Advanced Restore Options

I Select the location to which you want the selected files and folders to be restored – the original location, an alternative location or a separate folder. Click Next

Check out Windows XP Backup utility on the Microsoft website to find out more about these advanced restore options.

2 The next option allows you to choose how to deal with files that already exist on your computer – you may choose to leave them unchanged, to replace older files or to replace all files

3 The final Advanced restore option allows you to choose how to restore security and special system files

4 The Restore Wizard completion page will allow you to review the options selected. Click Back to change your selection

Completing the Restore

Click Next on the Wizard completion page to start the restore operation

2 The restore utility will locate the requested files from the backup and restore them to the specified location. A Restore Progress dialog box will appear as the restore operation begins

3 When the restore process is complete, click Close

4 Depending on the files you have restored, you may be prompted to restart your computer

If you keep a lot of important data on the computers in your home network it's well worth while to establish a backup routine to reduce the risk of losing data ... and then stick to it!

Securing Your Wireless Network

In this chapter we look at wireless home networking security, and you will learn how to ensure that your wireless home network is safe against unwanted attention or access, for example from drive-by hackers.

Security features such as Wired Equivalent Privacy and MAC filtering will be covered, as well as the latest security upgrades available under Wi-Fi Protected Access (WPA). We'll see how to upgrade your Windows XP to the latest Service Pack level to ensure you have all the latest security updates, and finally we'll look at ensuring security if you are remotely accessing your network.

Covers

Threats to Wireless Security | 114

What's at Stake? | 115

Wireless Security Best Practice | 116

Wi-Fi Protected Access (WPA) | 119

Downloading Windows XP Service Pack Updates | 120

Installing Windows XP Service Pack Updates | 122

Updating Wireless Adapter Drivers for WPA | 124

Securing Remote Network Access | 127

Chapter Eight

Threats to Wireless Security

Whether you're starting networking from scratch using wireless, or are upgrading an existing network with wireless components, you need to be aware that the great strength of wireless networking, namely its flexibility, is also a potential weakness.

Unlike a wired network, where you have to physically plug in to gain access, a wireless network broadcasts its traffic on the air and it's accessible to anyone with a wireless enabled PDA or computer.

War Driving

War driving takes its name from the movie "War Games", where hackers randomly dialed phone numbers until they found a modem.

This potential for easy access has inspired a movement known as "war driving", the practice of driving around with a wireless enabled laptop and an external antenna to identify and publicize the location of wireless networks.

A variant of this, "war chalking" emerged in London in 2002, with a set of symbols being chalked on sidewalks and buildings to identify access points.

let's warchalk..!	
KEY	**SYMBOL**
OPEN NODE	ssid / bandwidth
CLOSED NODE	ssid
WEP NODE	ssid access contact / bandwidth

blackbeltjones.com/warchalking

WEP vulnerability

Even if a network has been secured using WEP it may still be vulnerable, because the encryption method used in WEP was exposed early in its history as having cryptographic weaknesses.

Hackers can download software to crack WEP from the Internet!

The fact that the WEP encryption key stays unchanged unless manually reentered into every station in the network makes WEP vulnerable. WEP transmits information about the encrypting key as part of every data message and a determined hacker equipped with the necessary tools could collect and analyze transmitted data to extract the encrypting key. This requires several million packets to be intercepted and analyzed, but could still be accomplished in under an hour on a high traffic network.

The latest version of 802.11 security, Wi-Fi Protected Access (WPA) overcomes this vulnerability by providing for encryption keys to be changed automatically with time.

What's at Stake?

The types of security threats faced by a wireless network are many and varied. Here are just a few:

Insertion attacks
An attacker is able to connect to an access point without authorization because no password is requested.

Session hijacking
An attacker transmits false traffic into a connection and takes over the victim's TCP session.

Broadcast monitoring
In a poorly configured network, if the access point is connected to a hub rather than a switch, sensitive data packets not intended for wireless clients can be intercepted by an attacker.

ARP spoofing
An attacker can trick the network into routing sensitive data from a wired network onto the Internet, by accessing and corrupting routing tables.

Beware of any public hotspot that does not ask for your normal login information. Disconnect immediately!

Evil twin intercept
An attacker uses an unauthorized access point to trick wireless clients to connect and reveal sensitive data such as passwords.

Denial of service attacks
An attacker floods a wireless client with bogus data packets. This kind of attack is also much used in wired networks.

Jamming
An attacker floods the 2.4 GHz band with radio frequency interference, causing wireless communication to grind to a halt.

On a more mundane level, perhaps the worst that might happen is that you discover from your access log that the kid next door has been using your broadband Internet connection for free!

In most cases these types of attack require a high level of technical expertise on the part of the hacker, and they can be made that bit more difficult by ensuring that the full range of available security measures are enabled.

Wireless Security Best Practice

Wireless network security is seen as one of the main issues that is inhibiting wider uptake of the technology, and one that has resulted in a lot of critical press coverage.

The inherent vulnerability of the early 802.11b (Wi-Fi) security was recognized early on, but there are a number of steps that can be taken by anyone setting up a network that will give reasonable security against all but a determined hacker.

If you want to provide free public access to an Internet connection your security measures will be different. See page 140.

Change default SSID and disable SSID broadcast

Wardrivers in the US report that about 60% of all access points broadcast with their default SSIDs and that less than 25% have enabled WEP. Changing the default and, if your access point allows it, disabling the SSID broadcast are the first steps that will protect your network from idle snoopers.

See page 73 for an example of SSID disabling.

Use an administration password

Make sure that the setup function on your access point is password protected so that unauthorized users cannot gain access and change the security settings.

Enable WEP

WPA and upgrading older gear to WPA are discussed in the following sections.

Enabling WEP, using hard to guess keys and changing them regularly are important security steps. WEP will be progressively replaced by WPA (see next section) following the ratification of the IEEE 802.11i standard.

MAC address filtering

MAC address filtering allows you to secure your wireless home network by only allowing access to computers which have been registered on your access point.

A MAC or Media Access Control address is a 12 digit number that is unique to each network adapter. See page 78.

Use your AP's setup to enter allowed MAC addresses in the filter list. Keep the list up to date and delete any old entries

Use a firewall

Ensure that you have a firewall installed and enabled as a security barrier. If your wireless home network is connected to the Internet via a router then this is the place to install a firewall.

If you are using a laptop with a wireless adapter or built-in Wi-Fi to connect to a hotspot then enable the Windows Firewall on your wireless network connection or install another firewall product.

Windows Firewall was covered in chapter 6. Another product often recommended is Zone Alarm from www.zonelabs.com.

Consider manually assigning IP addresses

Although DHCP is easier to set up, manually assigning IP addresses to computers in your wireless network will prevent an unauthorized computer from obtaining an address automatically.

DHCP setup was covered on page 77. Select Disable if you want to assign IP addresses manually.

If you do decide to assign IP addresses manually, using a different set of private addresses rather than the default set for your access point will also keep would-be hackers guessing. For example the Linksys default set starts at 192.168.1.100. You can use any set in the private address ranges discussed on page 64.

Keep access points away from windows

Keeping your access point away from outside walls or windows will reduce the signal strength outside your home and limit the range at which unauthorized users might be able to detect and connect to your network.

Enable the log file and review access records regularly

Keeping a wireless access log will be one of the administrative functions of your access point. Enable the log and review its contents regularly to make sure any unauthorized access is identified.

Installing firmware updates may result in settings reverting to their factory default values.

Keep firmware up to date

Finally, as the manufacturer of your network equipment releases updated firmware and device drivers, download and install these so that your system is fully up to date with any security improvements.

Disable your wireless adapter when not in use

While your wireless network adapter is enabled, Windows XP will be constantly on the lookout for an access point or ad hoc connection matching one of the preferred network profiles you have defined.

It is possible for a hacker to set up a rogue access point matching one of your hotspot profiles. Disabling your adapter when you don't intend to connect will prevent attack by this route.

If the icon is displayed in your notification area you can also right-click this to access your network adapter.

Access your network adapter by opening the Network Connections folder from the Start menu or from the icon on your desktop

Right-click on the Wireless Connection and select Disable

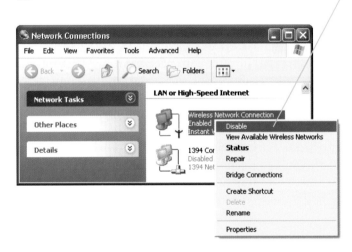

When you want to use the wireless adapter again, repeat these steps and select Enable

Wi-Fi Protected Access (WPA)

Wi-Fi Protected Access, or WPA, has been developed to overcome the known shortcomings in WEP described earlier. WPA is specified in the IEEE 802.11i standard that was ratified in June 2003 and provides new security features in four key areas.

Temporal Key Integrity Protocol (TKIP)
Encryption is mandatory under WPA, rather than optional as was the case for earlier 802.11 standards. TKIP changes the encryption keys and manages the synchronization of changing keys across the wireless network.

Michael
WPA improves previous integrity checks with a new 8-byte Message Integrity Code (the MIC in Michael). This is used to confirm that the data in a transmitted frame has not been tampered with.

Versions of WEP up to 256-bit are offered by some vendors, but these are not part of a standard and there is no certification of interoperability. In fact the longer keys give no significant additional protection.

Advanced Encryption Standard (AES)
AES replaces the WEP encryption with a new algorithm that uses 128-, 192- or 256-bit keys, compared to the 40-bit original WEP keys.

AES is optional within the new standard. This is because WPA is intended to be backwards compatible with earlier 802.11 devices but the new algorithm requires a new chip set and cannot be implemented as part of a firmware upgrade.

As WPA becomes widely adopted we will probably see authentication servers being added to the ever growing list of access point functionality.

User authentication
Authentication of users was optional for previous 802.11 versions but is required under WPA. Authentication can be via a pre-shared key or, for larger networks, via a dedicated authentication server.

Installing WPA
Although full implementation of WPA with certified interoperability has to await new hardware releases, many of the features can be implemented by installing free firmware upgrades to existing equipment.

An upgrade for Windows XP may also be required, as described in the next section.

Downloading Windows XP Service Pack Updates

To install the WPA update, your Windows XP must be upgraded at least to Service Pack 1 level.

Support for WPA is included in Windows XP with the Service Level 2 updates. If your Windows XP is also pre-SL1, you will need to install a Service Pack upgrade. In this section we describe the steps to download and install the Windows XP SP2 upgrade, which is available free from the Microsoft website.

Once you have upgraded you will also be able to find Windows Update in the Common Tasks Pane under Control Panel.

1 Start up Internet Explorer and type into the address field the URL windowsupdate.microsoft.com. The Windows Update Welcome page will load. Click Express Install

2 Express Install will identify the high priority updates needed by your computer. To view further information about each upgrade, click Details... Then click Install...

3 If requested, click to accept the end user license agreement for the updates you need to install

4 Windows Update will download the requested updates to your computer. This may take some time!

The Service Pack updates are large downloads and are also available as a free CD if you don't want to download them via your Internet connection.

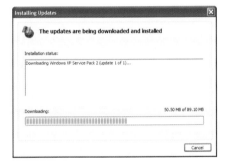

5 When the download is complete Windows Update will install the updates on your computer

Installing Windows XP Service Pack Updates

Once the Service Pack update download is completed the Windows XP Service Pack Setup Wizard will start.

To check the update level of your Windows XP version click Start, Control Panel, System. The Service Pack level is indicated on the General tab.

Backup your key data and close all programs before starting the setup. Backup is covered in chapter 7

2 The setup wizard will inspect your system and prepare for the Service Pack setup

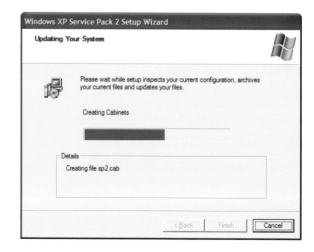

The setup wizard will check for available disk space before archiving files. If you don't have sufficient free space on your hard drive you will not be able to archive files.

3 After completing the setup, the wizard will give you the opportunity to enable future updates to be done automatically

4 Click Restart Now to activate the new Service Pack updates that have been installed

5 After restarting you will have the opportunity to manage your security settings using Windows Security Center

6 You can also access the Security Center later by clicking the icon in the notification area

Updating Wireless Adapter Drivers for WPA

To upgrade wireless equipment that did not originally include WPA, it is usually possible to download updated firmware or drivers from the manufacturers' websites.

Websites for other manufacturers will be different. There may be a specific download page for all products.

WPA upgrade for Linksys WPC11 wireless adapter

1 On the Linksys website at www.linksys.com, navigate to the WPC11 product page via Products, Wireless, Network Adapters. Click Drivers and Downloads

2 Click the link to start the updated driver download

This download is 16 MB. Some manufacturers may offer a free upgrade CD for customers who don't have a broadband Internet connection.

3 When prompted by Windows XP select Save, and in the next dialog box specify where to save the file on your computer

4 The new firmware will be downloaded and saved to the location you specified

Installing the driver upgrade

If your download comes in a ZIP archive you will have to extract files before the driver update can be installed.

1 Open Network Connections, right-click on your wireless network connection and click Properties

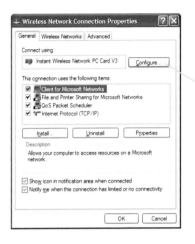

2 On the General tab click Configure...

3 In the Properties dialog box for your wireless network adapter select the Driver tab

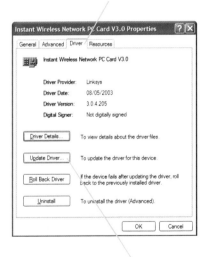

4 Click Update Driver... and the Hardware Update Wizard will start

You can also configure Windows Update to look for device drivers for you. Go to Control Panel, System, Hardware, Windows Update under Drivers.

5 Since you already have the upgraded driver, select "No, not this time". Click Next

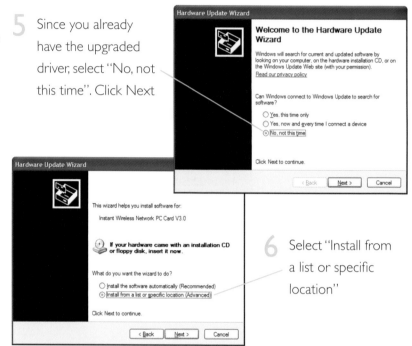

6 Select "Install from a list or specific location"

7 Navigate to the folder that contains the downloaded driver and click Next

Windows XP may warn you that the software has not passed Windows XP Logo testing. Click "Continue anyway" to go ahead with the update.

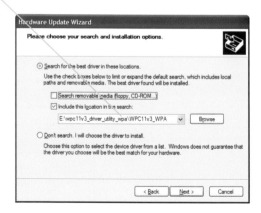

8 The wizard will locate the new driver and begin the update. Click Finish to complete the update

Securing Remote Network Access

In chapter six we saw how to set up a computer in your wireless home network as a remote access server, to allow you to log on to your network using a dial-up connection from a computer at a remote location.

Allowing incoming connections to your network is a potential security threat as it provides a route for someone to dial in to your modem and try to break in to your computer or network.

A few simple steps will ensure that this incoming connection remains secure.

Securing incoming connections

1 Click Start, Connect to, Show all connections

2 Right-click Incoming Connections and click Properties

3 Select the Users tab. Check the "Require all users to secure their passwords and data" check box

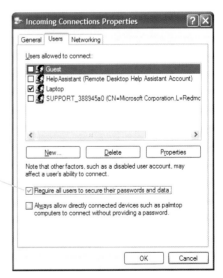

4 On the remote computer that you use to dial in to your network, click Start, Connect to, Show all connections. Right-click on the dial-up connection that you use to dial in and select Properties

5 Select the Security tab and select "Require secured password" from the drop down list under "Validate my identity as follows:"

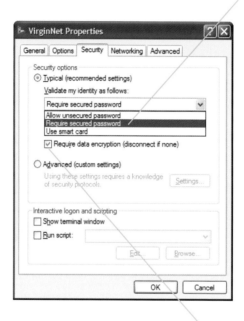

6 Check the "Require data encryption" check box. Click OK

Ensuring that user authentication and data encryption are required for computers that access your network via the incoming connection minimizes the threat to your network from this route.

Extending Wireless Network Range

In this chapter we'll take a look at extending the range of your wireless home network.

You'll learn about using external antennas to increase your wireless network range and about ways to extend your network with additional access points or by connecting two wireless networks together. We'll also take a quick look at community wireless networks.

Covers

Why Worry About Range? | 130

Making the Most of What You've Got | 131

Using an External Antenna to Increase Range | 132

Do-It-Yourself Antennas | 134

Wireless Network Bridging | 136

Community Wireless | 138

Chapter Nine

Why Worry About Range?

So far you've probably not been bothered by the question of the range of your wireless network – for surfing the Internet from your favorite armchair, or sharing files between computers in your home, it's not going to be an issue (unless your home is very big!)

But if you live in a house with thick stone walls, or you want to share your broadband Internet connection with your neighbors, then getting the most out of every milliwatt of transmitted power is going to be important to you.

The limit for the 2.4 GHz ISM band used by 802.11b gear is 1000 mW (in the US) or 100 mW (in the UK) of "equivalent isotropically radiated power" or EIRP. In the USA this limit is relaxed for high gain antennas.

In every country, national agencies specify the maximum power that can be transmitted in any radio frequency band, so it's not just a case of getting a more powerful transmitter.

Within the set limits, getting maximum range comes down to using a high gain antenna to increase your receiving sensitivity and to get your transmitted signal out as far as possible.

Antenna Basics

The two key characteristics of an antenna that you need to know about are its gain and radiation pattern.

Gain is a measure of how well the antenna increases effective signal power, and is measured in decibel units (dB). A convenient rule of thumb is to remember that an increase of 3 dB represents a doubling of power. Typical gains for Wi-Fi antennas are in the range of 3 dB to 20 dB.

The radiation pattern of an antenna tells you how much power goes in various directions relative to the antenna axis. The simplest antenna, radiating equally in all directions, has a so-called isotropic radiation pattern resembling the shape of a baseball.

Antenna manufacturers usually specify gain in dBi, which is dB relative to an isotropic antenna.

The highest gain antennas radiate energy predominantly in one direction and have a radiation pattern resembling a spotlight beam or a baseball bat.

Making the Most of What You've Got

There are some simple steps you can take before resorting to external antennas in order to get the best possible range from your current transmitter power and receiver sensitivity.

Avoid Obstacles

Out of doors, trees are a major problem, but only when they are in leaf!

1 Moving your access point away from a wall, or raising it higher off the ground, will improve its propagation pattern

2 Metal objects such as filing cabinets, furniture or shelving can also attenuate radio waves. Try to keep access points and receivers away from large metal objects

Adjust Access Point antennas

This is just like adjusting your TV aerial to get the best possible reception.

1 The signal strength from most access points will not be the same in all directions. Try adjusting the orientation of your AP and see if this improves signal strength at your receiver

2 If your AP has two adjustable "rabbit ear" or diversity antennas try aligning one antenna vertically and the other horizontally

Reorient your laptop

1 The transmitting power and receiving sensitivity of your wireless network adapter will also be strongest in one plane or direction. Changing the orientation of the adapter by facing in a different direction or tilting at an angle can give you better signal strength

Use an antenna enhancer

Some designs for antenna enhancers can be found on the Web – look at www.freeantennas.com.

1 If these steps don't give you the range you need, try an antenna enhancer, which improves antenna gain by adding a reflecting surface to the existing antenna on an access point

Using an External Antenna to Increase Range

If extending range is going to be important to you then you need to make sure when you buy your wireless gear that it allows you to connect an external antenna. This means either removable antennas in the case of an access point or a miniature connector in the case of a PC or PCMCIA card.

Several different types of antenna are available on the market, and the choice will depend on whether you want to increase sensitivity over a wide area or focus your transmitted power into a narrow beam in order to achieve maximum range in just one direction.

We'll look at the options, starting with wide beamwidth and narrowing down.

Omnidirectional Antennas

An omnidirectional antenna such as the Buffalo WLE-NDR has a gain of 2.5 dBi and a radiation pattern resembling a flat doughnut. It will increase your range over a wide area horizontally by reducing the amount of transmitted energy radiated vertically

A 3 dB gain gives a doubling of power at the receiver.

Patch Antennas

The patch antenna is more focused than the omni, with a forward pointing beamwidth of around 75 degrees. The Buffalo WLE-DA is an example of a patch antenna with a gain of 4 dBi

Directional Antennas

No, its not a sawn-off light sabre! Inside the protective housing is a directional Yagi antenna of the type that can give you maximum range and minimum beamwidth. The Buffalo WLE-HG-DYG shown here will give you a gain of 14 dBi (25 times the power compared to an

In the UK, the regulatory limits relate to power transmitted at the antenna, so if your transmitter is already close to the limit a high gain antenna can take you over the top. In the US, the FCC allows an increase in effective radiated power for high gain antennas, since their narrow beamwidth means they will cause less spurious interference.

isotropic antenna). This type of antenna is best suited to point-to-point applications, for example if you want to bridge between buildings or more remote locations. Parabolic antennas, like the common satellite dish, can achieve even higher gain and narrower radiation patterns than the Yagi

Connecting to a PC card

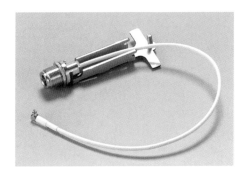

To connect an external antenna to a wireless adapter in a laptop you will need an adapter cable to convert from the connector on the PC card to the type-N or BNC connector on the antenna. An example of the type of connector is the Buffalo WLE-LNC illustrated here

Do-It-Yourself Antennas

Wireless networking may still be new technology, but it's quickly developing a folklore all its own, and a large part of that relates to the area of DIY antennas. This famously started with an antenna made by wireless networking pioneer Rob Flickenger from a Pringles can plus a few bits and pieces from the garage.

Commercial antennas are not particularly expensive but if you have a practical bent and get a kick out of a do-it-yourself approach to high tech this might be an interesting way to spend a spare evening.

Here are a few of the best sources of information.

The Original Pringles Can Antenna

You can read all about Rob Flickenger's original Pringles can antenna at www.oreillynet.com/cs/weblog/view/wlg/448

Lincomatic's Homebrew Wi-Fi Antenna Site

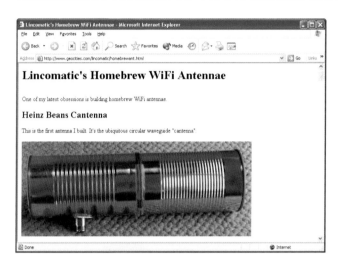

Lincomatic's Homebrew Antenna website shows examples of a range of DIY antennas, including omnidirectional and patch designs, as well as the cantenna shown above. You can find this site at www.geocities. com/lincomatic/homebrewant.html

The Double Quad and Patch designs are particularly effective and easy to build. The Patch is small enough to pop in your laptop case and can give you an added boost at a hotspot if you're just a little out of range

Another website worth taking a look at is www.netscum.com/~clapp/ wireless.html

Antenna Enhancers

As an alternative to a DIY antenna, an antenna enhancer adds a reflecting surface to the existing antenna, on an access point for example, to enhance the antenna gain. Some designs for enhancers can be found at www.freeantennas.com

Wireless Network Bridging

Connecting two physically separated networks using a wireless link is called wireless bridging. Most access points can also function as wireless bridges, and you can also buy dedicated devices that work as bridges only, connecting to similar devices but not to client computers.

Point to point mode

The simplest wireless bridge is a point to point connection between two wired networks. This might be a solution if you have wired networks in two nearby buildings that you want to connect without running an Ethernet cable between them.

Directional high gain antennas will give a big boost to a point to point connection.

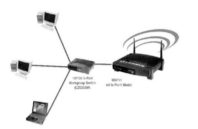

Point to multipoint mode

To connect more than two nearby wired networks you will need to use point to multipoint mode, where one access point or bridge is working as a central hub to route traffic between the other access points.

One AP should be configured in point to multipoint mode. The other APs should be in point to point mode. One AP is operating as a hub for the others.

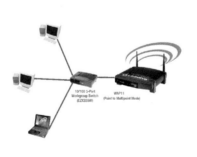
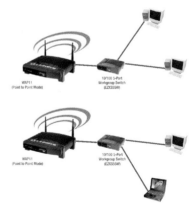

If you also want to connect individual computers wirelessly to any of the wired networks you will need a separate access point for that network, since an access point in bridge mode cannot also work as a normal access point connecting to wireless clients.

The exception to this is access point client mode which is an operating mode available in some vendors' access points.

Access point client mode

In this mode the MAC address of the main AP is entered into the client AP setup.

This mode allows you to extend the range of your wireless network by linking one access point to another, while each AP is also hosting other wireless clients in an infrastructure mode network.

Interoperability is likely to be an issue with access point bridging modes.

Stick to equipment from one manufacturer unless you are able to experiment before buying.

Last mile Internet access

One important application of wireless bridging is in extending the coverage of broadband Internet in areas where this is currently limited.

For example, a small community that is just out of range of a DSL enabled phone exchange could gain broadband Internet access by wireless bridging to an access point that is connected to the exchange, or an expensive satellite broadband connection could be shared across a community by bridging several wireless networks together.

Community wireless is covered in the next section.

Community Wireless

Interest in community wireless has been a major factor in the rapid growth in Wi-Fi over the last few years. Wireless networking is an inexpensive way of providing broadband Internet access to a community where a wired network would be impractical.

Community wireless projects are springing up around the globe, from Seattle and Somerset to Singapore and Sydney. There is a wealth of information on the Internet, including a helpful Get Started guide on the SeattleWireless.net site.

Setting up a community wireless project

1. Before you start, check the small print of your ISP agreement to make sure that sharing your broadband connection is permitted. If sharing is not mentioned, check with your ISP, and if you find it's not allowed then try shopping around for a more community friendly provider

2. The first step is to see whether your community shares your interest in wireless networking. Print some posters for local shops, libraries and schools. Drop some flyers into mail boxes and email your local radio, TV and newspapers to gauge the level of interest

3. Based on the response you receive you need to establish the area you want to try to cover with your community wireless network.

An external omnidirectional antenna with a few dB gain will extend this a little.

Microwave propagation programs are available which can check the suitability of antenna sites using local terrain maps.

If your site owners want to charge a rent then you'll have to factor this into your overall project costs.

You'll find sample constitutions and antenna site owner agreements on the Internet, for example at www.wlan.org.uk.

The advertised open air range of an access point will be in the range of 1000 to 1500 feet. Choose a conservative figure and map out how many access points you need to cover your area

4 Walk around your community and identify suitable sites for your external antennas. The main criterion is good line-of-sight visibility to your target area but a remote hill top may not be ideal as you'll also need a power connection

5 Consider the wireless bridging options covered in the previous section if your target area extends beyond the range of a single access point

6 Talk to the (hopefully community spirited) owners of the sites where you'd like to put your antennas and get their OK

7 Next do the sums! Plan and cost all the gear you need for the project, plus any rents and broadband Internet costs. Share the setup and ongoing costs information with your community group and agree how these costs are going to be covered

8 Setting up a constitution for the group may seem unnecessarily formal, but will provide a clear and agreed basis for resolving any later disputes

9 Order and install your access points and antennas, and assist users with wireless adapter installation and setup

10 Test all equipment on-site. Check wireless coverage with a wireless enabled laptop or PDA. The Netstumbler program, available from www.netstumbler.com has a useful signal to noise readout for checking wireless signal strength

Hold your official opening. Secure the services of a local celebrity and get plenty of publicity from local media

Security for community wireless projects

Many of the security issues for a community wireless project will be similar to those for a private infrastructure mode wireless network that we discussed in chapter 8.

The key issue that your group will need to decide is whether the service is limited to paid-up members, or whether, once the basic setup and running costs are covered, other users within the community will be allowed free access.

Members only: If your group decides to keep the shared service closed, then all the security measures discussed in chapter 8 can be applied: disabling SSID broadcast, enabling WEP, registering the MAC addresses of members and so on.

In addition, all members should enable firewall software either using the Windows Firewall or another firewall product, in order to protect themselves from unwanted attention from the Internet.

Open access service: On the other hand, if your group decides to allow free access to anyone in the community, these security measures will not be applied. You will want to broadcast the SSID and disable WEP, MAC address filtering and so on.

The firewall issue remains, and as organizer of the group it will be helpful of you to advise and assist other users in setting up this feature.

Community wireless administration

Whichever model your group chooses, you should ensure that the access point administration function is secure by setting an administrative password.

Enabling the log file and regularly reviewing the log file records will also give you a good idea of network usage, and alert you to any unauthorized access if you're running a members only service.

You may want to change the SSID to reflect the name of your community project.

As well as Internet connection sharing, Internet telephony might be an interesting service to consider as part of a community project. Check out the information at www.skype.com.

Wireless Hotspot Networking

In this chapter we'll look at connecting to the Internet through a Wi-Fi hotspot.

Some of the main hotspot services in the USA, the UK and internationally are introduced, and you'll learn about aspects of security that you should be aware of when using hotspots.

Covers

Introducing Wireless Hotspots | 142

Finding a Hotspot | 143

Connecting to Hotspot Services | 144

Hotspots in the USA and Canada | 145

Hotspots in the UK and Europe | 149

International Hotspots | 152

Hotspot Security | 154

Chapter Ten

Introducing Wireless Hotspots

Wi-Fi hotspots are public access points where the connection between a mobile computer and the Internet is made using a wireless link.

Driven by large international telecoms operators as well as small local enterprises, hotspots are springing up by the tens of thousands worldwide. In partnership with venue owners, the early focus is on hotels, airports and coffee shops, with names like Starbucks, Hilton and Borders at the front of the pack.

Some estimates put the number of hotspots in the US at half a million by 2007, up from only 4000 at the end of 2002.

Hotspots enable you to connect to the Internet or, often using a secure VPN connection, to your corporate network when you're out and about.

Getting started

To get started using wireless hotspots you need a portable computer – a laptop, a notebook or even a PDA – equipped with a wireless network adapter card.

Then you need to find a hotspot location. The service providers' websites that we'll look at later in this chapter provide directories of their own sites, and there are a number of independent directories that give global coverage.

Some pay-as-you-go services only let you connect to the hotspot at which you first sign up.

Some of the limitations

The hotspot industry is still in its infancy and one of the things that has yet to develop is a comprehensive cross-charging system to allow users to roam between hotspot operators.

At the moment if you buy access with one operator you can usually only use that operator's hotspots. However, consumer demand is driving progress in this area, and with companies such as iPass and Boingo focusing on aggregation it looks as if true global roaming across Wi-Fi hotspots may be on the horizon.

The technology to allow roaming between Wi-Fi hotspots is also "work in progress" following the ratification of the IEEE 802.11f standard.

Security is also an issue you need to be aware of when using hotspots. We'll cover this in detail later in this chapter.

Finding a Hotspot

Wireless hotspots are being established by a number of telecoms and other operators in a wide range of locations all around the world. The initial emphasis is on business travelers, with hotspots located in airport lounges, hotels and major rail stations.

The more casual user is catered for by the partnerships springing up between telecoms operators and venues such as coffee shops and pubs.

A good place to look for hotspot locations is at the wifinder website www.wifinder.com.

Several other hotspot directories are listed in chapter 12 (see page 180), and you can also check out the websites of the main hotspot providers:

- T-Mobile   www.t-mobile.com
- Surf and Sip   www.surfandsip.com
- Swisscom Eurospot   www.swisscom.com
- Boingo   www.boingo.com
- BT Openzone   www.bt.com/openzone

Connecting to Hotspot Services

Some operators bundle hotspot Internet access in with phone or home broadband charging. Look out for an offer from your phone or broadband operator.

Hotspot providers offer a variety of subscription options, ranging from short term access for perhaps a couple of hours up to monthly or annual subscriptions. For your first experiments with hotspots you may want to sign up for short term access.

The initial steps to connect to a hotspot are the same for all operators and are covered below. In the following sections you'll see the sign-up procedures of some of the major hotspot operators in more detail.

Initial steps to connect to a hotspot

Don't get too comfortable until Windows XP has connected to the hotspot with at least a good or very good signal strength. If you're in an area with low signal strength you may have to move! Alternatively, if your wireless NIC has an antenna connector, check out the DIY antenna designs in chapter 9.

1 Find yourself a comfortable seat in the coffee shop, hotel lobby or airport lounge and switch on your laptop. Right-click the Wireless Zero Configuration icon in the notification area

Click View Available Wireless Networks

Don't leave your laptop unattended when you go to get a newspaper or some extra sugar. It might not be there when you get back.

2 Select the hotspot service you want to connect to from the list of networks and click Connect. Windows will warn you that you are connecting to an unsecured network

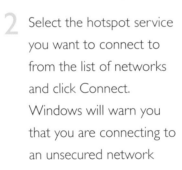

If you are using a browser other than Internet Explorer and have trouble reaching the login page, try again using IE.

3 Start up your Internet browser. Your browser's Home Page request will be redirected to the welcome page of the hotspot service provider

4 Follow the steps in the following sections, or on the welcome page for the particular hotspot that you're connecting to

Hotspots in the USA and Canada

There are over a hundred hotspot operators in the US and this number is likely to grow in the near future, although some shake-out and consolidation seems likely in the longer term. We'll take a quick look at a few of the major operators.

T-Mobile hotspots
A division of Deutsche Telecom, T-Mobile is becoming a major player both in the USA and in Europe, although service offerings vary by region.

At www.t-mobile.com/ hotspot/ follow the Sign Up link for information on various service options

The T-Mobile Connection Manager is an easy to use tool to manage all your wireless connections, including T-Mobile hotspots.

Take care when entering your credit card or other confidential data in a public place. Make sure no one's looking over your shoulder.

Create a new account online, sign up using a promotional offer or add Wi-Fi to your existing account if you are already a T-Mobile customer

A T-Mobile subscription can be used at over 12,000 hotspot locations worldwide.

With over 5,300 locations across the US at airports, and in partnership with Starbucks and Borders, T-Mobile operates two-thirds of all US hotspots

AT&T Wireless hotspots

AT&T's hotspots are available at a large number of airports, hotels and resorts in 50 major cities across the USA.

The AT&T wireless site at www.attwireless.com gives full information on connecting, service plans and so on

You can buy AT&T's Connect service online in advance or at any hotspot location.

The step-by-step sign-up procedure depends on the service plan you wish to purchase

Check the Wi-Fi Service Hotspots link to get the latest information on available locations by region

Verizon Wireless hotspots

Verizon is currently providing free hotspot access at locations in New York to existing customers. If the trial in NY is successful, Verizon plans to extend its Wi-Fi coverage to its other major East Coast markets.

At www.verizon.net/ wifi/ follow the Getting Connected link for information on connecting to a Verizon hotspot

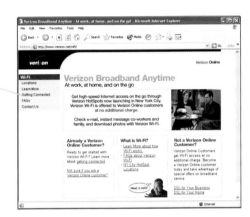

Click Locations for up to date information on the available hotspot locations in New York

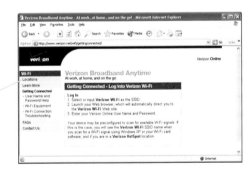

For information on other hotspots in New York take a look at:

- http://www.downtownny.com, and
- http://publicinternetproject.org

Wayport hotspots

Wayport is a leading hotspot provider in the USA and is pioneering roaming alliances, for example with AT&T, iPass, Boingo and GRIC. This may help pave the way for cross charging arrangements that will allow hotspot users to roam between service providers and not be tied to a single hotspot operator or location.

Find information on service plans and pricing from the Wayport Home Page at www.wayport.net

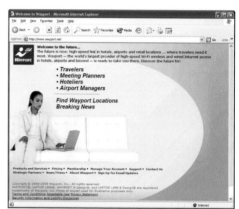

FatPort: Canada

FatPort is Canada's largest public Wi-Fi operator, with locations across the country. See www.fatport.com.

FatPort has a roaming agreement with Airpath (US), Kubi Wireless (Spain), NetWireless and Oasis Wireless (Canada) and SwissCom (International)

Other hotspot operators in Canada include Oasis Wireless (www. oasiswireless.net) and NetWireless (www.netwireless.ca).

Hotspots in the UK and Europe

Hotspots are being rapidly established in the UK and across Europe by a number of operators in partnership with venue owners. Check out www.wifinder.com for the latest on locations.

T-Mobile hotspots

In Europe, T-Mobile is setting up hotspots in partnership with Starbucks:

Buy yourself a nice Grande Latte, Double Espresso, or whatever is your favorite beverage, find a comfortable seat and follow the steps on page 144. This will bring up the T-Mobile home page

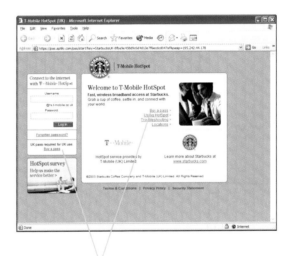

Make a note of the Username and Password in case there is an interruption in your connection before you can access the confirmation email.

Click Buy a Pass either from the central menu or from the login panel on the left, and follow the sign-up procedure

When you have completed the sign-up you can use the links on the Your Session dialog to find other T-Mobile locations or to troubleshoot your connection

Surf and Sip hotspots

Operating in Europe in partnership with Internet Exchange cafés.

1   Find yourself a comfortable seat and follow the initial steps described on page 144. This will bring up the Surf and Sip welcome page

2   If you have purchased a prepaid access card, enter the card number as it appears on the back. Otherwise, click Sign Up! and you'll be asked to select a service plan

3   Once you have created an account and entered your payment details, click Login and this will take you back to the welcome page. Enter the Username and Password you chose when creating your account

Make a note of the Username and Password in case there is an interruption in your connection before you can access the confirmation email.

4   When you have logged in successfully your browser will load the surfandsip.com home page. You can now start to surf the Internet

BT Openzone hotspots

BT Openzone is building a hotspot network in the UK together with Hilton Hotels, UK airports and Costa Coffee.

1 Find a comfortable seat and follow the initial steps described on page 144. When your browser starts up this will take you to the BT Openzone welcome page.

2 Select "Create a new account" from the menu on the left

3 Once you have created an account, log in and click the Top Up My Account link to buy your Internet Access pass

Other European hotspot operators

Elsewhere in Europe, check out:

- www.orange-wifi.com and www.kasteurope.net in France
- www.monzoon.net in Germany and Switzerland
- www.hubhop.com and www.winq.com in the Netherlands
- www.aptilo.com in Denmark
- www.swisscom.com for hotspots throughout Europe

International Hotspots

The rest of the world is not being left behind in the hotspot stakes, with a wide variety of local enterprises as well as the major international operators starting hotspots.

If you're traveling for business or vacation and want to stay connected, take your laptop and wireless adapter along with you.

Australia: Azure Wireless

A 2002 start-up with hotspots in hotels, convention centers, cafés and airports starting in Melbourne and Sydney, and now extending across Australia.

Azure and Boingo have a global roaming agreement

Hong Kong: Systech Telecom

A Hong Kong start-up that operates hotspots in hotels and shopping centres around the island.

Systech offers free wireless adapter hire at hotel receptions for hotel guests.

Free access is available at some of the shopping mall locations. Prepaid cards can be purchased at hotel receptions

Singapore: StarHub

A local operator with a network of 300 hotspots covering Suntec City, Changi Airport and The Coffee Bean and Tea Leaf outlets.

StarHub has a global roaming agreement with iPass and GRIC

Malaysia: Maxis

Maxis hotspots, called Utopia WLAN Zones, can be found at a large number of cafés, restaurants, hotels and other venues around Kuala Lumpur and Petaling Jaya.

Maxis also offers VPN and a low cost voice over IP (VoIP) phone service

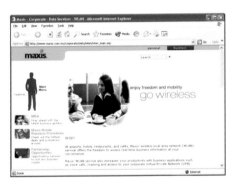

Philippines: Airborne Access

A March 2002 start-up that is quickly building a hotspot network in major cities in the Philippines, partnering Netopia Internet Cafés and Seattle's Best coffee shops.

Japan has a wide network of free hotspots. See the site listings from www.wifinder.com or www.wififreespot.com for info.

The site also offers a helpful guide to setting up the most popular wireless adapters

Hotspot Security

Wireless Network security is covered further in chapter 8.

To make hotspots easily accessible for public users, hotspot operators generally disable the security features such as data encryption that are available for wireless networking.

This means that most communications from your computer such as web based email will be transmitted as clear, unencrypted text and may be vulnerable to illicit interception.

Although it may seem unlikely that hackers would target hotspot users, there are a number of measures you should consider taking in order to ensure that your data and resources are as secure as possible.

Using a Personal Firewall

A variety of personal firewall products are available, including several freeware downloads. They can protect you as a hotspot user from the action of other users and also make you aware of any malicious applications that may try to access your resources.

Windows XP's Firewall is covered on page 88.

Information on personal firewalls can be found at www.firewall.com

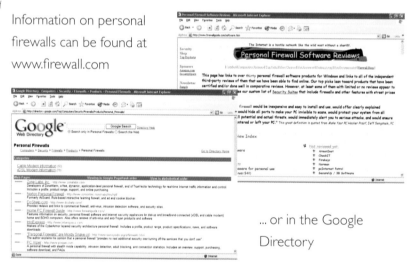

... or in the Google Directory

Make sure your personal firewall and antivirus software are enabled and keep them up to date with the latest upgrades.

Using Antivirus Software

Antivirus software will protect your resources from the effects of viruses and other "attack vectors" that may attempt to infect your computer from the network. Perhaps equally importantly this type of software could save you the embarrassment of infecting other computers that you may connect to.

Apply the latest Windows Service Packs

You can either use Windows XP's automatic update service or else connect directly to the Windows Update website to download the latest operating system updates and service packs.

Keeping your system up to date will improve its performance as well as security. See page 120.

Windows XP upgrades and service packs can be accessed from the Microsoft website at http://support.microsoft.com

Watch out for SSL Security

If you connect to a secure site, your data will be encrypted using secure socket layer (SSL) technology.

SSL is the current standard method for encrypting secure transactions across the Internet.

You can recognize a secure Internet site either by the https:// address in your browser address window ...

Check with your email service provider to see if they offer a secure email service.

... or by the locked padlock in the notification area in the bottom right of the browser. You will usually see https:// being used when you provide credit card details, or change your password or other confidential data. Don't trust a site to be secure if you don't see these

Hotspot service providers generally recommend not to use web based email to transmit confidential information and if possible to encrypt any email attachments before sending them.

A hotspot provider's VPN service may secure the wireless connection, but sensitive data could still be vulnerable when routed on from the hotspot provider. Consider encrypting sensitive data unless the VPN connection goes all the way to your data's destination.

VPN security

Some hotspot operators offer the security of a Virtual Private Network or VPN connection.

Keep sensitive passwords secure

If you have passwords to sensitive information on your computer don't reuse these on hotspots where your user information may be transmitted unencrypted and therefore open to eavesdropping.

Disable your wireless adapter when not in use

If you are using your laptop in the open but not connected to a hotspot, then it is good practice to disable your wireless adapter.

1. Right-click on the Wireless Network Connection icon in your notification area. Click Disable

2. To re-enable your Wireless Adapter later, repeat step 1 and click Enable

Don't auto-connect to non-preferred networks

It is possible for a hacker to set up a bogus access point that looks to your computer like a bona-fide hotspot. Depending on your Wireless Zero Configuration settings your computer may automatically associate with the access point, providing a possible entry route to your computer.

1. Open Network Connections and double-click your Wireless Network Connection. On the Wireless Networking tab click the Advanced button

2. Uncheck the "Automatically connect to non-preferred networks" check box

3. Click Close and OK

Troubleshooting Your Home Network

Even if you have carefully followed all the steps in the previous chapters, it's probably only a matter of time before you hit the unexpected.

In this chapter we'll look at how to troubleshoot your wireless home network, starting with the process of trying to pin down the source of the problem. Then we'll cover problem symptoms you may encounter with the various elements of your network, and possible solutions.

Finally, we'll look at the network diagnostic tools available in Windows XP and MS-DOS.

Chapter Eleven

Covers

First Analyze the Problem | 158

Troubleshooting Network Adapters | 160

Troubleshooting Network Resource Hosts | 162

Troubleshooting Network Connections | 163

Wireless Interference | 164

Troubleshooting Internet Connection Sharing | 165

If Wireless Zero Configuration is Not Available | 166

Checking Network Connectivity | 168

Other DOS Diagnostic Tools | 171

Diagnostics Using MS Help and Support Center | 173

First Analyze the Problem

The first step in troubleshooting any networking problem is to use some common sense to try to track down its cause.

For example, if you are trying to access a file on another computer in your network, then for this to work you must have:

A working connection means both that the physical link works (e.g. the wireless signal is strong enough) and that the software works (e.g. that the necessary protocols are installed).

- a network adapter, properly installed and configured, in your computer

- a working connection to your network hardware such as hub, switch or access point

- a working connection from this hardware to the other networked computer

- a properly installed and configured network adapter in the other computer

- the file you're trying to access enabled for file sharing

You may find it helpful to make a sketch of your network connection, and then check off each element as you confirm that it's working properly. Don't forget the software as well as the hardware.

Troubleshooting process

1. If you are unable to reach any resources on your network then the problem may be with your network adapter or its configuration. You may get this kind of message:

You may still get this message for a few seconds after making a wireless connection. Try to access the network resource again after a few seconds.

Start with the section Troubleshooting Network Adapters on page 160. Come back to step 2 if your adapter checks out OK

2. Use the DOS "ping" command to do a loopback check on your network adapter. See the section Checking Network Connectivity on page 168 to learn how to do this

3 If your adapter seems OK, then the next thing to check is network connectivity. You may get this kind of warning if your connection is down:

> i) **Could not reconnect all network drives**
> Click here to open My Computer and see the status of your network drives.

Use the DOS ipconfig command to check that your computer has a valid IP address assigned to it. See the section Other DOS Diagnostic Tools on page 171 to learn about ipconfig

Use the ipconfig command to find the address of another computer, or use your default gateway IP address (see page 171) to ping your Internet gateway.

4 Check that your computer can "ping" other devices on the network. See the section Checking Network Connectivity on page 168 to learn how to do this

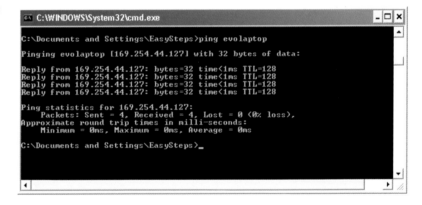

```
C:\WINDOWS\System32\cmd.exe

C:\Documents and Settings\EasySteps>ping evolaptop

Pinging evolaptop [169.254.44.127] with 32 bytes of data:

Reply from 169.254.44.127: bytes=32 time<1ms TTL=128
Reply from 169.254.44.127: bytes=32 time<1ms TTL=128
Reply from 169.254.44.127: bytes=32 time<1ms TTL=128
Reply from 169.254.44.127: bytes=32 time<1ms TTL=128

Ping statistics for 169.254.44.127:
    Packets: Sent = 4, Received = 4, Lost = 0 (0% loss),
Approximate round trip times in milli-seconds:
    Minimum = 0ms, Maximum = 0ms, Average = 0ms

C:\Documents and Settings\EasySteps>_
```

It will also help your diagnosis if you can check whether other computers on the network have a similar problem accessing the network resource.

5 If your computer and network connection seem OK then perform the same checks from the computer you are trying to reach, to ensure that its adapter and connection are working correctly

If these steps do not identify the problem, check out the MS Help and Support Center (see page 173) or the troubleshooting websites listed on page 185.

Troubleshooting Network Adapters

If it looks as if the problem is with a particular network device, check its physical installation and its configuration and then run the Windows Hardware Device Troubleshooter.

Check the physical installation

If the connection that you are troubleshooting is not in Network Connections, the adapter may be disconnected. For example if it's a USB device it may have been unplugged.

1 Check that the device is correctly inserted or plugged in, that it's powered up (if applicable), and that any necessary cables are also properly plugged in

2 Open Network Connections. Check that the network connection is not disabled or disconnected

Local Area Connection 2
Disabled
Realtek RTL8139 Family PCI F...

Local Area Connection 2
Network cable unplugged
Realtek RTL8139 Family PCI F...

If an adapter has been switched off or ejected from its PC slot it may be necessary to restart the computer to get the adapter to restart correctly.

3 If the device is disabled, right-click the connection icon and click Enable

Check the device configuration

1 Double-click the network connection that you're troubleshooting

2 On the General tab, check that all the needed items are installed

See page 60 to install any missing items

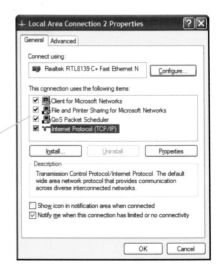

3 Click Configure in the Properties dialog box for this connection. The Properties dialog box for the adapter will open

It's worthwhile checking on the manufacturer's website to make sure you have the latest version of the driver and firmware for your adapter.

The device Properties box will indicate whether the device is working properly

4 If the device is not working properly click Troubleshoot... to start the Hardware Device Troubleshooter

If your hardware comes with a manufacturer's diagnostic program you can also use this to test the device.

If none of these checks reveals the problem you could also try removing your network adapter and reinstalling it, connecting it to another computer, checking the manufacturer's website for any driver updates or compatibility issues, or searching on Google or the troubleshooting websites listed on page 185.

Troubleshooting Network Resource Hosts

On the computer that's hosting the resource you're trying to reach, you should also check that the network adapter is properly installed and configured.

1 Check that the host computer is switched on and also that its network adapter is enabled. Open Network Connections on the host computer and examine the status of the network link from both ends

If one or other computer has been switched off and on again, interrupting a wireless link, try switching off both computers and restarting. The wireless link should re-establish itself automatically.

2 If the configuration of the host computer's network adapter has changed since the connection was established, other computers in the workgroup may need to be reconfigured to match

3 For a wireless network, if WEP enablement has been changed on one computer, network communications will not work and you will not be able to "ping" another computer. Follow the steps at the end of chapter 3 (page 41) to update WEP on other computers in the network

4 Confirm that the sharing status of the file, directory or other resource has not been changed since the last time it was accessed (See page 51)

Shared Music

5 Check that the target file or directory has not been moved since the Network Place was set up. Windows gives a warning if an attempt is made to move a shared file or directory

If you are unable to see a computer that was previously accessible as part of your workgroup then as a last resort rerun the network setup wizard and redefine your workgroup (see page 46).

Sharing

You are sharing C:\Documents and Settings\EasySteps\My Documents\EasySteps as EasySteps. The folder will not be shared after you move or rename it. Are you sure you want to continue?

Yes   No   Cancel

Troubleshooting Network Connections

If your network adapter checks out, the next thing to verify is the physical link to your network hub, switch or access point.

1 Check that cables are properly connected and do not show any physical damage. If possible, test a suspect cable in another part of the network

If you are in the habit of disabling your wireless adapter when it's not in use, check that the adapter is enabled when you are ready to use the wireless link again.

2 For an infrastructure mode network, verify that the connection parameters such as the SSID have not been changed on either the host or remote computer, or on the access point

You will have a different format for this dialog box if you have updated your Windows XP with Service Pack upgrades (see page 122).

3 Similarly for a peer-to-peer connection, verify that the properties for the connection are identical at both ends. Make sure that if WEP is enabled, the check box for "The key is provided for me automatically" is unchecked

If the View Available Wireless Networks dialog box is grayed out, see page 166.

4 If a wireless connection is intermittent, check for any sources of interference (see page 164) or try moving closer to the access point or to the other computer in a peer-to-peer connection

Wireless Interference

The 2.4 GHz ISM band used for Wi-Fi communications is also used by a wide variety of other devices, from microwave ovens to garage door remote controllers and cordless phones.

If you experience reduced data speed on your wireless connection, or hear pops and crackles on your cordless phone, it could be due to interference between different devices.

The so-called "collision avoidance" algorithm used for Wi-Fi means that interference will not cause you to lose data, but it will cause lots of data frames to be retransmitted, slowing down transfer rates.

Try any or all of the following steps to minimize or eliminate interference.

Interference with cordless phones

 Bluetooth wireless devices also use the 2.4 GHz band and will cause performance degradation in the vicinity of a Wi-Fi network. The IEEE 802.11 and 802.15 standards groups are working to alleviate this problem.

 Direct Sequence and Frequency Hopping are two methods of coding digital data onto radio signals. Wi-Fi uses the Direct Sequence method.

 Keep your access point at least 10 feet away from a microwave oven.

1 Check to see whether your phone is a Frequency Hopping or Direct Sequence device

2 If it's a Direct Sequence device, try operating your access point or ad hoc link on another channel. Try channels 1 or 11 at either end of the ISM band. See page 73.

3 Change the position of your access point, or the cordless phone base station. Try to maximize separation between these devices

4 If you have the option, connect an external antenna to the wireless network adapter. A high gain antenna with a narrow beamwidth is less sensitive to interfering signals coming from outside its radiation pattern

5 If none of these measures is effective then junk the cordless phone, try to get one that operates on another frequency band, or consider upgrading your wireless network gear to 802.11a (Wi-Fi5) on the 5 GHz band (see page 19)

Troubleshooting Internet Connection Sharing

If Internet Connection Sharing (ICS) has been enabled (see chapter 6, page 84) but you are unable to control the connection from a network computer, check the ICS setup.

Unable to remotely control an Internet connection

This warning may be displayed when you try to control the connection from a network computer:

You may also find that the Internet Gateway icon is no longer present in the Network Connections folder, despite network control of the connection having been previously enabled.

Check that network control of the connection has not been disabled on the host computer. On the host computer open Network Connections, right-click the icon for your dial-up Internet connection and select Properties and then Advanced. Ensure that the "Allow other network users ..." check box is checked and click OK

2 If the checkbox was unchecked in step 1 then try again now to control the Internet connection from the network computer. Otherwise try restarting the ICS host computer

If Wireless Zero Configuration is Not Available

The option to View Available Wireless Networks comes up when you right-click the Windows XP Zero Configuration icon in the notification area.

When trying to connect to a wireless network using Windows XP Wireless Zero Configuration, you may find that no networks are shown in the Wireless Network Connection dialog box after selecting View Available Wireless Networks.

The Wireless Zero Configuration Service is a piece of software that Windows needs in order to create and configure wireless connections.

This will occur if the Wireless Zero Configuration service has been turned off. Follow these steps to restore the service

Right-click My Computer on your desktop or Start menu and select Manage

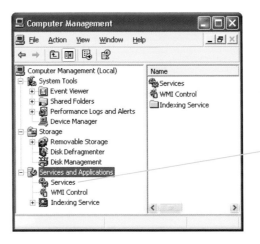

2 Expand Services and Applications and then double-click Services

...to Wireless Zero Configuration and

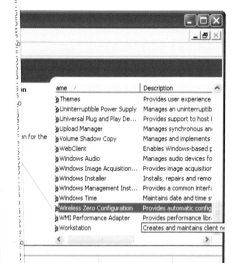

...ation dialog box click Start and ...service

The Connect to Wireless Network dialog box will now be active and you will be able to select the network you want to connect to

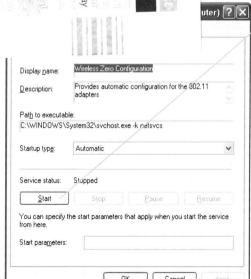

Checking Network Connectivity

If you have trouble reaching another computer on your network, the place to start is to check that all the plugs, cables and removable network adapters are properly installed.

A problem with wired network connections may be indicated in Network Connections as shown here, where a disconnected network cable is indicated.

If all the cables check out then there are a number of tools available to test your network adapter and its connectivity across the network to other computers.

Check your network adapter using the Ping test

Ping tests network connectivity by sending a data packet called an echo request to the indicated IP address and timing the echo response.

1 Open a DOS prompt window by clicking Start, Run. Type "cmd" in the Open field and click OK

2 In the DOS prompt window type "ping 127.0.0.1"

This IP address (127.0.0.1) is a reserved address that points to the network adapter on the host computer. Testing the network adapter in this way is called a loopback test. You can also type "ping localhost" or "ping name", where name is the name you gave to the computer you are checking when you set up your network.

```
C:\WINDOWS\System32\cmd.exe

Microsoft Windows XP [Version 5.1.2600]
(C) Copyright 1985-2001 Microsoft Corp.

C:\Documents and Settings\EasySteps>ping 127.0.0.1

Pinging 127.0.0.1 with 32 bytes of data:

Reply from 127.0.0.1: bytes=32 time<1ms TTL=128
Reply from 127.0.0.1: bytes=32 time<1ms TTL=128
Reply from 127.0.0.1: bytes=32 time<1ms TTL=128
Reply from 127.0.0.1: bytes=32 time<1ms TTL=128

Ping statistics for 127.0.0.1:
    Packets: Sent = 4, Received = 4, Lost = 0 (0% loss),
Approximate round trip times in milli-seconds:
    Minimum = 0ms, Maximum = 0ms, Average = 0ms

C:\Documents and Settings\EasySteps>
```

3 Four echo request packets are sent and the return times are shown if the test is successful. If you get the message "Request timed out", the receiving network adapter is not responding to the echo requests

If your network adapter passes the loopback test the next step is to check connectivity to other computers on your network. The ping test will do this for you too.

To ping another computer you need to know the computer's IP address. If the computer is in your local network you can also use the computer name.

Pinging another computer

You can also find the IP address of a computer from the DOS prompt by typing "ipconfig /all". See page 171.

To find the IP address of a computer, open Network Connections, right-click the Local Area or Wireless Network connection and

expand the Details section on the task pane. The IP address is shown here

Notice that the IP address here is allocated by the Windows XP Automatic Private IP Addressing service (APIPA). See page 63.

Open the DOS prompt window as described on the last page. Type "ping IP address", where IP address is the address of the computer you want to test connectivity to. You can also ping the name of the computer if it is in your local network

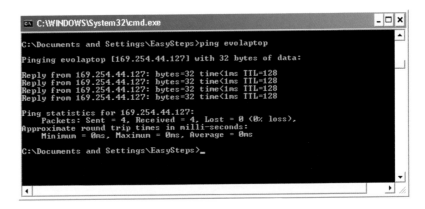

Here the connectivity check to the target computer was successful

Diagnosing unsuccessful ping tests

A "Request timed out" or a "Destination host unreachable" message indicates that the ping test to a remote computer was not successful.

"Request timed out" indicates that the echo request packets were sent out but no response was received. The problem may be with the remote computer:

IP addressing will not be a problem if the APIPA service is used.

- the IP address is incorrect
- the computer is off or has crashed
- the network adapter is not working properly
- the computer has a firewall enabled on this connection

The problem may also be with the host computer or elsewhere in the network:

It is not advisable to enable a firewall such as Windows Firewall on internal network connections, only on the connection to the Internet at an ICS host or Internet gateway.

- host computer has incorrect IP address or subnet mask
- an interconnecting hub or switch is not working

A "Destination host unreachable" message indicates that the host computer or some intermediate routing device is unable to contact the remote computer. This may be because:

- the host computer is disconnected from the network
- your router is disconnected from the network
- an intervening router is disconnected

There are a number of options that you can use with the ping command to gather more information. To see these options just type ping in the DOS prompt window without an IP address.

The problem may also indicate that a router does not have any information on how to route traffic to the address that you are trying to ping.

Other DOS Diagnostic Tools

There are a number of other tools that can be invoked from the DOS prompt that can help you trace any problems with network connectivity.

Ipconfig

Ipconfig gives you the basic IP configuration information for all the network adapters connected to your computer

```
Command Prompt

Microsoft Windows XP [Version 5.1.2600]
(C) Copyright 1985-2001 Microsoft Corp.

C:\Documents and Settings\EasySteps>ipconfig

Windows IP Configuration

Ethernet adapter Local Area Connection 2:

        Media State . . . . . . . . . . . : Media disconnected

Ethernet adapter Wireless Network Connection:

        Connection-specific DNS Suffix  . :
        Autoconfiguration IP Address. . . : 169.254.186.233
        Subnet Mask . . . . . . . . . . . : 255.255.0.0
        Default Gateway . . . . . . . . . :
```

Type "ipconfig /?" at the DOS prompt to see the full list of command options.

Some ipconfig command options can disrupt your network connection, for example by releasing automatically assigned IP addresses. Take care here!

The option "ipconfig /all" gives you further detailed configuration information on your network adapters, such as MAC addresses and DHCP status, as well as host configuration information

```
Command Prompt

C:\Documents and Settings\EasySteps>ipconfig /all

Windows IP Configuration

        Host Name . . . . . . . . . . . . : Study
        Primary Dns Suffix  . . . . . . . :
        Node Type . . . . . . . . . . . . : Unknown
        IP Routing Enabled. . . . . . . . : Yes
        WINS Proxy Enabled. . . . . . . . : Yes

Ethernet adapter Local Area Connection 2:

        Connection-specific DNS Suffix  . :
        Description . . . . . . . . . . . : Realtek RTL8139 Family PCI Fast Ethe
rnet NIC
        Physical Address. . . . . . . . . : 00-40-05-7A-AA-40
        Dhcp Enabled. . . . . . . . . . . : Yes
        Autoconfiguration Enabled . . . . : Yes
        Autoconfiguration IP Address. . . : 169.254.227.178
        Subnet Mask . . . . . . . . . . . : 255.255.0.0
        Default Gateway . . . . . . . . . :

Ethernet adapter Wireless Network Connection 3:

        Connection-specific DNS Suffix  . :
        Description . . . . . . . . . . . : Instant Wireless USB Network Adapter
 ver.2.6 #2
        Physical Address. . . . . . . . . : 00-06-25-19-96-49
        Dhcp Enabled. . . . . . . . . . . : Yes
        Autoconfiguration Enabled . . . . : Yes
        Autoconfiguration IP Address. . . : 169.254.186.233
        Subnet Mask . . . . . . . . . . . : 255.255.0.0
        Default Gateway . . . . . . . . . :

C:\Documents and Settings\EasySteps>
```

Netstat

Netstat displays information about all the active connections on your computer

Type "netstat /?" at the DOS prompt to list the command options.

Tracert

Tracert traces the route through the network to the destination computer or URL that you specify

Type tracert at the DOS prompt to see the list of command options.

You can specify the destination you want to trace as an IP address, a local name or a URL

Diagnostics Using MS Help and Support Center

The Microsoft Help and Support Center, accessible from the Start menu, includes a Network Diagnostics tool that will run a series of tests on your computer and its network connections and report back whether your system passes or fails each test.

Using the Network Diagnostics tool

1 Click Start, Help and Support, and under "Pick a task" click "Use Tools to view your computer information and diagnose problems"

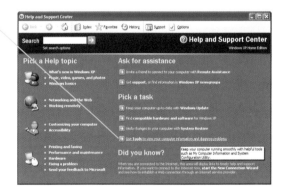

2 In the Tool pane on the left, click Network Diagnostics

3 In the next dialog box you have two options, either to "Set scanning options" or to "Scan your system"

Click "Scan your
system"

4 Network Diagnostics will scan your system and report back a list
of information gathered on each item tested

The list shows
whether network
components have
passed or failed the
diagnostic tests

5 Click on the + button beside each element in the list to view
further details of the diagnostic information gathered

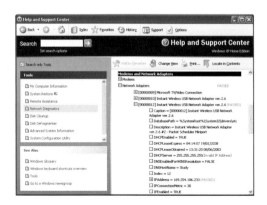

Further Information Sources

Wireless home networking is a fast moving area with a wealth of information available online, from technical aspects of hardware and software to information about organizing community wireless LAN projects.

Here you'll learn about some of the most useful websites to keep you up to date with the latest developments on the home wireless networking scene.

Covers

General Networking | 176

Wireless Networking | 178

Hotspot Directories | 180

Community Wireless | 181

General Wireless Topics | 182

Offbeat Wireless Topics | 183

Buying Wireless Home Network Gear | 184

Network Troubleshooting | 185

Chapter Twelve

General Networking

Sites listed here give general information to help with setting up home networks and background information on networking technology and new developments.

www.homenethelp.com

This is a site dedicated to helping home network users at the beginner and intermediate level.

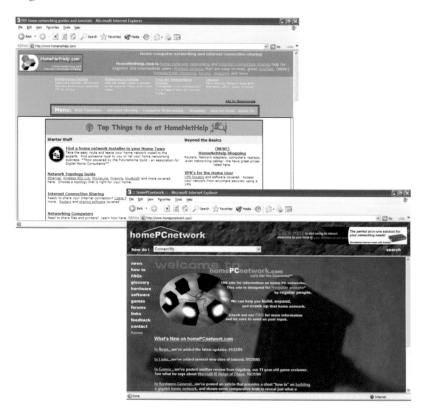

www.homepcnetwork.com

Home PC Network provides practical coverage of everything related to Personal Computer networks.

Other home network information sites worth visiting:

- www.linuxhomenetworking.com
- www.homenetnews.com

If you want to find out about home networking options that are no-new-wires rather than truly wireless, take a look at these sites, which deal with the technologies we looked at in chapter 1.

www.homeplug.org

Homeplug.org will give you the low-down on using your power circuits as a no-new-wires networking solution.

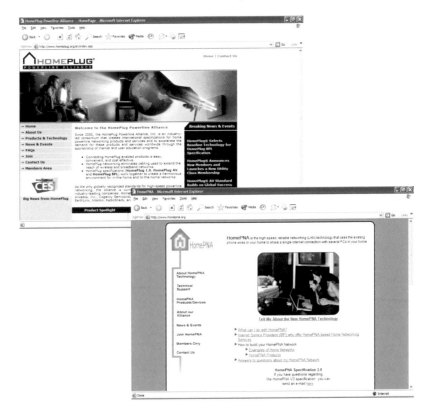

www.homepna.org

Homepna deals with all aspects of the technology that uses your existing phone lines to provide a no-new-wires solution for home networking.

Wireless Networking

www.practicallynetworked.com

Practically Networked gives practical help on wireless networking, with product reviews and step-by-step help.

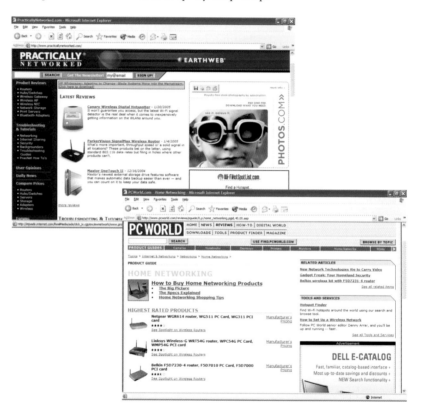

www.pcworld.com

The wireless section of PC World's site contains news, reviews, how-tos and downloads on wireless networking.

Other sites worth checking out

The websites of the main wireless networking equipment vendors sometimes have general information. Try also:

- www.wifinetnews.com
- www.openwlan.com

www.wi-fi.org

The Wi-Fi Alliance is a nonprofit association formed to certify interoperability of 802.11 based wireless networking products. Like some of the other official organizations dealing with Wi-Fi and other wireless networking topics, it has an informative site.

See also the general networking sites listed on page 176, which cover an increasing range of wireless networking topics.

www.getnetworked.co.uk

Although this site is allied to Linksys, the advice it gives is applicable to equipment from all manufacturers.

The Network Wizard will help you to identify the gear you need, based on the devices you want to connect up to your network.

Hotspot Directories

As well as the www.wifinder.com site introduced in chapter 10, there are a number of other sites that will help you find out about hotspot availability in your area.

www.wififreespot.com
This site lists free hotspots around the world.

www.hotspotlist.com
A directory of US and international hotspots, although the international coverage has some way to go to match wifinder's.

Other hotspot information sites worth checking out:

- www.wi-fizone.com
- www.hotspot-hotel.com
- www.jiwire.com
- www.hotspotting.org

Community Wireless

You'll find a lot of sites on the Internet covering community wireless networking. They'll give you a wealth of information about setting up your own community project and about many other wireless networking topics.

www.seattlewireless.net
Seattle Wireless is a not-for-profit group developing a wireless broadband community network in the Seattle area.

www.communitywireless.org
Community Wireless is an umbrella organization representing the needs of the emerging community networks.

Other community wireless sites worth a look include:

- www.freenetworks.org
- www.airshare.org
- www.broadband-wireless.org

General Wireless Topics

A quick search on Google will reveal thousands of sites dedicated to all aspects of wireless computing and networking. Here are a few of the most useful.

www.wi-fiplanet.com

This is a complete guide to the world of 802.11 wireless, with news, reviews, features and tutorials.

www.wireless.com

Wireless.com is a knowledge center on all things relating to wireless and mobile computing.

Other wireless information sites worth checking out include:

- www.dailywireless.org
- www.wirelessweek.com
- www.wirelessinternet.com

Offbeat Wireless Topics

Wireless networking is a young and fast moving area of new technology that has not yet left its geeky origins completely behind. These offbeat sites give an insight into those origins.

www.wardriving.com

Their ongoing mission is to seek out access points and unsecured wireless networks, and alert us all to the security issues!

www.wardrive.net

Find out here all about wardriving, warchalking and what they mean for the security of your wireless network.

Here are a few others on a similar theme:

- www.warchalking.us
- www.netstumbler.org
- www.homenetnews.com

Buying Wireless Home Network Gear

You may end up at eBay or Amazon when you've decided what you want to buy. To get you to that point here are a few sites that will help you find the right equipment for your network.

www.pcmag.com
See the websites of PC Magazine and its rivals for product reviews of all the latest networking and wireless equipment.

www.whatpc.co.uk
You'll also find excellent hardware reviews and much more on this site, as well as at www.zdnet.com.

Other sites worth looking at before you buy your gear are:

- www.tigerdirect.com in the USA
- www.outpost.com in the USA
- www.wirelesspro.co.uk in the UK
- www.qtds.com in the UK

Network Troubleshooting

The Microsoft Help and Support Center may be your first port of call for troubleshooting information, but there's a lot out there on the Web too.

www.pcpitstop.com

This site has a range of resources covering network troubleshooting under Windows and lots more to help keep your PC tuned-up.

See also www. windows networking. com for other helpful articles on troubleshooting.

www.annoyances.org

Annoyances.org contains information put together for and by Windows users. See the Troubleshooting articles for solutions to many networking problems.

www.practicallynetworked.com/support/troubleshoot-wireless.htm

This website contains extensive troubleshooting suggestions on setup and configuration, WEP, drivers and other topics.

www.microsoft.com

And for the "official" view, try searching the Windows XP networking troubleshooting pages at www.microsoft.com/windowsxp/using/networking/getstarted/troubleshoot.mspx.

Index

A

Access point 20, 24
    Access point client mode 136
    Adjusting antennas 131
    Bluetooth 14
    Extending range 130
    Firmware upgrades 76
    Functions 66
    Location 68, 131, 164
    Log file 76
    Mixed mode 73
    Network bridge 25
    Point to point mode 136
    Print server function 25
    Rogue hotspot 118
    Selecting 24
    Switch function 25
    Wireless network bridging 136
Access point configuration
    Advanced options 77
    Channel selection 73
    Configuration utility 71
    Dynamic routing (RIP) 82
    Installation 69
    Internet connection 72
    MAC address cloning 75
    Multicast pass through 76
    Port forwarding 80
    Remote management 76
    Restoring factory defaults 75
    Router log 76
    Routing 81
    Security settings 74
    SSID 73
    WEP setup 73
    Wi-Fi mode 73
Administration password
    Access point setup 74
    Changing default 116
Advanced Encryption Standard
    WPA feature 119
Ad hoc mode 30, 37
    Creating new connection 39
    Security 41
Antennas 11
    Antenna basics 130
    Antenna enhancers 131, 135
    Beamwidth 132, 164
    Directional 133
    Diversity antennas 131
    DIY antennas 134
    External 164
    Gain 130
    Omnidirectional 132
    Patch 132, 135
    PC card connection 133
    Pringles can antenna 134
Antivirus software 154
    Hotspot security 154
    Internet connection firewall 89
APIPA 169, 170
    Selecting in network setup 63
ARP spoofing
    Security threat 115
AT&T 146

B

Backup
    Advanced backup options 106
    Advanced restore options 111
    Backup to CD 104
    Daily 106
    Differential 106
    Incremental 106
    Installing Windows Backup utility 101
    Restoring backed up data 109
    Running a backup 103
    Selecting files to backup 104
    Setting backup schedule 107
    Specifying backup destination 105
Backup or Restore Wizard 103
Beamwidth
    And interference 164
    Extending range 132
Bluetooth 14
    Wi-Fi interference 164
Boingo 143, 152
Bridging 24
Broadcast monitoring
    Security threat 115
BT 143, 151

C

Community wireless
  Administration 140
  Antenna sites 139
  Last mile Internet 137
  Online information 181
  Security 140
  Setting up a project 138

D

Data rate 10, 15
  Bluetooth 14
  HomePlug 13
  HomePNA 12
  IrDa 14
  Viewing ICS connection speed 87
  Wireless connection status 38
Denial of service attacks
  Security threat 115
DHCP
  Access point function 66
  Access point setup 77
  With Internet filters 79
  With port forwarding 81
  With private IP addresses 64
Diagnostic tests
  Ipconfig 171
  MS Help Network Diagnostics 173
  Netstat 172
  Ping 168
  Tracert 172
Directional antennas 133
DOS commands
  Ipconfig 159, 171
  Netstat 172
  Ping 168
  Tracert 172
Drive sharing 55
Dynamic routing (RIP)
  Access point setup 82

E

Email
  Hotspot security 154
EIRP
  National Regulations 133
Evil twin intercept
  Security threat 115
Extending range
  Access point location 131
  External antennas 132
  Network adapter antenna connector 133
  Wireless bridging 136

F

Fast User Switching
  Remote network access 96
Fatport 148
File and folder sharing 51
File and Printer Sharing
  Remote access 96
File and printer sharing
  Enabling during network setup 49
Firewalls
  At hotspots 154
  Security best practice 117
  Troubleshooting 170
Firmware
  Security updates 117

G

Games console adapter 26
Gateway
  Internet 24

H

Hardware Device Troubleshooter 161
HomePlug 13
  Online information 177
HomePNA 12
  Online information 177
HomeRF 15
Home Media Servers 27
Hotspots
  Connecting to a hotspot 144
  Finding a hotspot 143
  Getting started 142
  Security 154
Hotspot operators
  AT&T 146
  Boingo 143
  BT 143, 151
  Fatport 148
  International 152
  Online directories 180
  Surf and Sip 143, 150
  Swisscom 143
  T-Mobile 143, 145, 149
  Verizon 147
  Wayport 148

I

IEEE standards
  802.11a 19
  802.11b 18
  802.11f 142
  802.11g 18, 164
Incoming connections
  Security 127
Infrared connections 13
Infrastructure mode
  hannel sensing 33
  Setup steps 67
Insertion attacks
  Security threat 115
Interference 163, 164
  Access point location 68
  Troubleshooting 164
Internet connection 47
Internet Connection Sharing
  Connecting using ICS 86
  Disconnecting using ICS 87
  ICS host settings 84
  Monitoring using Windows Task Manager 98
  Troubleshooting 165
  Viewing ICS status 87
Internet filters
  Access point setup 79
Internet telephony 140
Interoperability 21
  And network bridging 137
Ipconfig command 159
  Troubleshooting 171
IP addresses 62
  Access point setup 70
  APIPA 63
  In ICF log file 91
  Private addresses 63
  Specifying in network setup 62
  Subnet mask 64
IrDA 13

J

Jamming
  Security threat 115

K

Key
  Changing WEP keys 114
  WEP enabling peer-to-peer connections 40

L

Loopback test
  Network adapter testing 168

MAC address
    Access point setup 75
    MAC address filtering 78, 116
Mapping a shared drive 56
Media center PC 28
Michael
    Message Integrity Code 119
Microsoft Help and Support Center 96
Music system adapter 26
My Network Places
    Arrange icons 59
    Sharing resources 58

Router 69
Network performance
    Using Windows Task Manager 98
Network resources
    Folder and file sharing 52
    Printer sharing 53
Network setup 46
Network setup disk
    Creating 49
    Running on other computers 49
Network Setup Wizard 46
New Connection Wizard 93
New Hardware Wizard 35
No New Wires
    HomePlug 13
    HomePNA 12
    Introduction 12

Netsetup 50
Netstat command
    Troubleshooting 172
Netstumbler
    Signal strength checker 139
Network adapters 11, 20
    For desktop computers 22
    For laptop computers 21, 23
    Games console 26
    History using Windows Task Manager 98
    Home media server 27
    Installing 31, 35
    Installing driver upgrades 125
    Monitoring performance 100
    Music system 26
    Troubleshooting 160, 168
    Updating drivers for WPA 124
    Video camera 26
Network address translation
    With private IP addresses 64
Network bridging
    Access point client mode 137
    Interoperability 137
    Point to point mode 136
Network connections
    Internet gateway 86, 165
    Remote access connection 93
    Troubleshooting 163, 166
Network diagnostics tool 173
Network hardware
    Online information 184

Omnidirectional antennas 132

Parabolic antennas 133
Patch antennas 132
Peer-to-peer connection 30
    Connecting to existing 37
    Creating a new connection 39
    Security 41
Performance
    Creating a log file 100
    Windows XP Performance program 99
Ping command 162
    Checking network connectivity 168
    Diagnosing ping tests 170
Port forwarding
    Access point setup 80
Printer sharing 53
Private folders 52
Protocols 60
    Access point installation 70
    Adding network connection items 60
    Definition 10
    In ICF log file 91
    TCP/IP 60, 62, 70

Radio frequency spectrum 11
Remote access
  Security 127
  Setting up remote access 93
Resource sharing
  Troubleshooting 162
Restore
  Advanced Restore options 111
  Restoring backed up data 109
Routing 20
  Access point setup 81
  Log file and security 117
  Routing table 82

Security
  Best practice 116
  Disabling network adapters 118, 156
  Firewall 117
  Manual IP addressing 117
  Peer-to-peer connections 41
  Remote access security 127
  SSL 155
  User authentication 128
Service Pack Setup Wizard 122
Session hijacking
  Security threat 115
Sharing Resources 51
  Allowing others to change 51
  Drives 55
  Enabling during network setup 49
  Files and folders 51
  File and printer sharing services 60
  Mapping a shared drive 56
  Network printer setup 54
  Printers 53
  Private folders 52
  Remote access 96
  Renaming or moving shared resources 52
  Share name 51, 53, 56
Signal strength
  Access point location 68, 131
  Antenna enhancer 131
SSID
  Changing default 33, 116

Configuring a network adapter 33
  Disabling broadcast 116, 140
Streaming video 27
Surf and Sip 143, 150
Swisscom 143

T-Mobile 143, 145, 149
  Connection manager 145
TCP/IP 60
Temporal Key Integrity Protocol
  WPA feature 119
Tracert command
  Troubleshooting 172
Troubleshooting
  Destination host unreachable 170
  Hardware Device Troubleshooter 161
  Internet Connection Sharing 165
  Ipconfig 171
  MS Help and Support Center 159, 173
  Network adapters 160
  Online information 185
  Problem analysis 158
  Request timed out 170
  USB devices 160

USB
  Access point configuration port 71
  Bluetooth printer adapter 14
  External IRDa port 13
  Network adapters 23
  Troubleshooting USB devices 160
User authentication 128
User Permissions
  Remote access setup 95

Verizon 147
Video camera adapter 26
VPN
    Access point settings 74
    At hotspots 156
    Remote network access 95

War chalking 143
    Online information 183
War driving 114
    Online information 183
Wayport 148
WEP
    Enabling 116
    Passphrase 73
    Peer-to-peer connection 37, 41
    Troubleshooting 163
    WEP vulnerability 114
Wi-Fi Alliance
    Online information 179
Windows 98/2000/ME
    Installing network adapters 31
    Shared folder name 51
    Shared printer name 53
Windows Firewall 88
    Changing log file size 90
    Community wireless security 140
    Diagnosing network connectivity 170
    Enabling Windows Firewall 88
    Logging dropped packets 89
    Logging successful connections 89
    Monitoring Internet traffic 91
    Viewing the log file 90
Windows Security Center 123
Windows Task Manager
    Monitoring network performance 98
Windows Update
    Downloading SP updates 120
    Updating adapter drivers 126
Windows XP 8
    Backup and restore utility 101
    Installing network adapters 35
    Logo testing 126
    Media Center Edition 28

Service Pack updates 120
    Updating for WPA 120
Wireless bridging 136
Wireless networking
    Advantages 9
Wireless Zero Configuration 30
    Connecting to peer-to-peer connection 37
    Troubleshooting 166
Wizards 125, 162
    Add Printer 54
    Backup or Restore 103, 109
    Hardware Update 125
    Network Setup 46, 67
    New Connection 93
    New Hardware 31, 35
    Service Pack Setup 122
Workgroup
    Network printer setup 54
Workgroup name
    On other network computers 49
    Specifying in network setup 48
WPA 119
    Installing WPA 119
    Updating adapter drivers 124
    User authentication 119
    WEP vulnerability 114